Social Development Through Benevolent Business

Social Development Through Benevolent Business

Kalyan Sankar Mandal

BEP BUSINESS EXPERT PRESS

First published in 2018 by
Business Expert Press, LLC
222 East 46th Street, New York, NY 10017
www.businessexpertpress.com

ISBN-13: 978-1-63157-672-0 (paperback)
ISBN-13: 978-1-63157-673-7 (e-book)

Business Expert Press Environmental and Social Sustainability for Business Advantage Collection

Collection ISSN: 2327-333X (print)
Collection ISSN: 2327-3348 (electronic)

Cover and interior design by S4Carlisle Publishing Services
Chennai, India

First edition: 2018

10 9 8 7 6 5 4 3 2 1

Printed in the United States of America.

Dedication

Tirtha
Samya
Debashree
&
Saurav

Abstract

This book points out that apart from usual "profit maximizing business," there exists other types of business models whose primary goal is to serve social causes and not just profit maximization. However, as we are schooled under the self-interest serving nature of human beings under capitalism, we are generally oblivious about the not-so-common existence of business models aimed at serving social goals.

The book discusses with examples, business models that aim at serving social goals in a self-sustaining manner. Thus, the business models discussed in this book are social business, compassionate business, microfinance-based business, cooperative business, business aiming at "Bottom of the Pyramid," and social welfare business. The common point of all these business models is that they promote benevolence to society through business, which is not necessarily true for an usual profit maximization business. All these business models alleviate poverty and promote social development in a self-sustaining manner. The book identifies the main principles followed by these business models and based on the principles identified, it suggests a unique business model which we call as "benevolent business model." Thus, through this book, the students not only become aware and acquainted with the winning principles of social purposes-serving business models, most importantly, they will also get an idea about how to design a successful benevolent business.

The author argues that along with the government and the NGOs, which are presently expected to meet social developmental needs, benevolent businesses should be promoted for meeting social developmental needs of the people, particularly of the poor.

Keywords

Benevolent business, Bottom of the pyramid business, Compassionate business, Cooperative business, Microcredit based business, Profit maximization business, Social business, Social development, Social welfare business.

Contents

Preface

As a researcher in social sciences, I became interested in probing on how poverty can be eradicated. Thus, I was engaged in studying the poverty-eradication programs undertaken by the government of India, which constituted an important part of its programs for socio-economic development. I studied the government's programs of poverty alleviation as it is widely believed that poverty alleviation is primarily the responsibility of the government. I found that the government's programs of poverty alleviation had very limited accomplishment. For instance, I found that often the nonpoor misappropriated the assistance meant for the poor. This finding was not very uncommon. What was intriguing that, at times, despite delivering assistance to the poor, the poor could not get income out of that assistance and instead, the nonpoor benefitted from the processes of providing assistance to the poor. As primarily, the government was entrusted with the task of alleviating poverty, this did not show much hope and the light at the end of the dark tunnel. I was looking for a way out. It was at that point that I heard C. K. Prahalad's assertion about "poverty alleviation with profit." I got intrigued. I started wondering, can a business earn profit and, at the same time, eradicate poverty? I wondered, can there be a business aiming at eradicating poverty? Or is it possible to eradicate poverty through business? Soon, I came across the concept of "social business" articulated by Muhammad Yunus, which aims at eradicating poverty and promoting social development through business. I became fascinated with that idea. I started probing. Thus started my journey, which resulted in this book.

Kalyan Sankar Mandal
Kolkata
January 2018

Acknowledgments

I was engaged in giving shape to a song for more than a year. While composing the song, I realized that the different tunes that I have listened to for some time now were getting mixed in the song that I am composing. At times, I was not able to distinguish the sources very clearly. Thus, I do not claim any originality at all in composing this song. And I am indebted and apologetic if I have failed to acknowledge the sources duly. The composition was facilitated by many. I mention some below.

The Indian Council for Social Science Research, New Delhi awarded a Senior Fellowship, which enabled me to undertake this work. The Centre for Studies in Social Sciences, Calcutta under the Directorship of Professor Tapati Guha-Thkurta provided me the affiliation and facilitated this work.

I got an opportunity to take part in the shaping of Nutrimix Social Business, through my association with the NGO, Child in Need Institute (CINI). Dr. Samir Chaudhuri, the Founder and Secretary of CINI, provided me this opportunity, which was helpful in shaping my ideas for this work.

My students, both of Fellowship (PhD) and Postgraduate (MBA) Programs, at the Indian Institute of Management Calcutta, were co-travelers in the shaping of my thoughts in this book.

And finally, going through Nobel Laureate Prof. Muhammad Yunus's writings and listening to his talks were influential in shaping of my ideas for this book.

I express my gratitude to all of them.

CHAPTER 1

Introduction

Business and Social Development

How is "business" related to poverty alleviation and social development? According to one school of thought, the expansion of business activities leads to the generation of employment and income thus, contributs to the removal of poverty and promots social development. A business may pursue the goal of earning profits. However, this very process may indirectly contribute to poverty alleviation and social development. On the contrary, critics of this school of thought point out that the expansion of a business may generate income and wealth to only those who own the business or form the capitalist class, and does not help in removing poverty. According to these critics, in a capitalist society, business involves the exploitation of the working class by the owners of the business or the capitalist class. Thus, the rich become richer and the poor become poorer, resulting in inequality, poverty, and other social problems. Set in this backdrop of conflicting thoughts, this book will discuss *a different type of business*, a business aiming at poverty alleviation, solving social problems, and promoting social development, while also seeking profits.

It is commonly assumed that promoting social development is one of the primary responsibilities of the government. Apart from the government, nongovernmental organizations or NGOs also contribute in promoting the development of the society. However, the NGOs are seen to play only a limited role in promoting social development in comparison with the government. We put forth the fact that apart from the government and the NGOs, some forms of businesses can also play a key role in alleviating poverty and promoting social development.

In capitalist societies, the primary goal of a business is to earn and maximize its profits. Hence, it is difficult to imagine how such a business with the goal of maximizing its profits could contribute to removing poverty and promoting social development. In this context, it is often argued that the profit-maximizing goal of the business exploits workers, causing poverty unfortunately.

On the other hand, we argue that not all businesses aim at only maximizing their profits. Furthermore, profit-maximizing businesses need not be the only type of business that exists today. A comforting fact is that there are some types of businesses that also aim at promoting social development. We are not referring to merely economic development, but are also referring to development in a much more broader sense that we will term as "social development." Thus, in proceeding with this viewpoint, an introduction to the forms of businesses that aim at social development and an elaboration of the concept of social development are required.

1.1   Business Models for Social Development

Businesses provide goods and services to their customers for an amount of money. Meanwhile, they earn a profit out of such transactions and also focus on maximizing their profits. In capitalist societies, most commonly, a business is privately owned. At times, in capitalist societies, the state may own a business to provide goods and services to its people. Though, in general, profit maximization is the main goal of any business, the state may, at times, run a business primarily to serve a social cause.

However, despite serving a social cause, any business needs to be profitable to exist without hassles. To set up a business, one needs capital. Businesses, most commonly, raise their capital by selling shares in the market. In the light of selling shares, a business needs to make a profit so that it would be in a position to give dividends to its shareholders. Thus, businesses strive to maximize their profits, so that they can provide higher dividends to their shareholders. This is the most widespread concept behind conducting a business in a capitalist society. Thus, in a capitalist society, a business needs to be and is run with the goal of profit maximization.

Now, let us look at another perspective. Usually, the government and the NGOs are the entities engaged in promoting social development.

As the government and the NGO sectors do not compete in the market, they are usually run less efficiently than the businesses that face stiff competition.

It has been unfortunately observed that businesses run efficiently, so as to be able to thrive amidst high competition in the market, are not engaged in any form of social development. If only the efficiently run businesses focus on promoting social development as well, then social development outcomes are likely to be better. We also find that businesses primarily being exposed to the high competition in the market and, hence, run efficiently for survival are likely to be more capable of promoting social development as compared with the government and the NGO sectors.

Capitalism assumes that human actions are guided by narrow self-interest. However, we agree with Yunus (2008, 39–40) in pointing out that this assumption whereby human beings are only governed by self-interest is not entirely correct. Although self-interest impacts human beings majorly, they also are capable of acting in ways to serve others. This concept is highlighted by the way NGOs aim to cater to the people.

Nonetheless, we are of the opinion that organizations can be run with the goal of serving a social purpose too. Also, in the process of serving society, they have the prospects of remaining competitive, being profitable, and generating surplus and thus, being run in a self-sustaining manner. These organizations are examples of businesses of a different form. They vary markedly from the businesses that are concerned only with maximizing profits. For these organizations, the primary goal is serving a social cause while also being able to generate profits, which helps them to remain successful. It must be kept in mind that profit-making is not the primary goal of these organizations, but generating a surplus is equally important for their sustenance.

We have discussed some examples of these types of businesses. By calling them a business, we highlight the fact that being self-sustaining is as much a main goal to them as is serving society. These businesses serve society through their operations, while also generate a surplus for self-sustinance or more. Among such businesses, there are various types. There is the example of a "social business," which primarily aims at serving a social cause in a self-sustaining manner. Any profit earned does not go to any individual, but is made use of to serve the social cause better (Yunus 2008, xvi). Furthermore, there is an example of a "business focusing on compassion" which tends to serve a social cause. For this, they resort to novel innovations and framing appropriate policies enabled them to serve the social cause more efficiently in a self-sustaining manner, while also generating a profit. Then, there is the example of a micro-enterprise sought by the poor to make use of the microcredits to alleviate their poverty. Here, the business aims at alleviating poverty by enablining the poverty-struck owners of the business generate an income. There are also examples of "cooperative business," which often aim at alleviating poverty by forming cooperatives. Moreover, there exist businesses that aim at maximizing profits like any other enterprise, but also orient their business strategy to provide goods and services to those who are at the "bottom of the income pyramid" (BOP) or are poor. This enables them to earn a profit and alleviate poverty as well. Also, there are examples of "social welfare business" providing welfare services to the society, while conducting business in the regular manner for profit.

Thus, we argue that there exist certain types of businesses that are different from businesses maximizing their profits alone. Such businesses that care for the underprivileged too not only serve a social cause, but are also able to generate a profit to help keep themselves self-sustaining. We will be discussing examples of this particular type of businesses and show how these businesses are capable of promoting social development through self-sustinance or profit.

1.2   What Is Social Development?

Although in the literature of the social sciences, the day-to-day vocabulary of the layman, and in the promises made by politicians, the term "development" is often used, the real meaning of the term is not always very comprehensible. The term "development" has been defined and redefined time and again. Below I mention some of the instances of defining development.

Most commonly, economic growth, expressed as the increase of per capita income, is taken as the most important indicator of development by the economist (Ingham 1993, 1803). One important advantage of taking economic growth as an indicator of development is that it can be easily measured. Thus, it is possible to compare the growth of the economy of one particular year with that of the previous years. Similarly, the rates of growth of different countries can be compared and some judgment can be passed on whether a country is developing or not. That is why economic growth remains an important criterion in understanding development.

However, it was sooner or later realized that economic growth by itself is not the best indicator of development. Development necessitates that economic growth is accompanied by some other types of growth changes such as technological transformation of agriculture, industrialization, urbanization (Hunt 1989, 61), growth of bureaucratic organizations, shift from authoritarian to more democratic structures, and a changing focus from religion to a more scientific and secular worldview (Ingham 1993, 1806). Often these criteria have been taken into account to depict modernization of a society (Singh 1973, 191). Thus, development implies both economic growth as well as "modernization" of the society giving due importance to the above-mentioned criteria.

In the late 1970s, the perception of development was broadened further. Indicators of development were not just growth and modernization. Apart from growth and modernization, emphasis shifted to include redistributive growth or growth-with-equity as well. A redistributive growth of income and wealth was considered as desirable for development (Arndt 1983, 1). In other words, meeting the basic needs of the people became one important concern of development (Hunt 1989, 262).

However, subsequently, redistributive growth was not the sole focus. Terms such as "capabilities" and "entitlements" of people were also emphasized on (Sen 1983, 745). Thus, it has been argued that development should not only incorporate a redistributive growth of income, but also allow all citizens to obtain access to basic amenities of life such as education, health care, income, and employment (UNDP 1992, 2). Soon, emphasis shifted from economic development to overall human development.

Ever since the publication of the World Commission on Environment and Development (Brundtland Commission) Report, the concept of sustainability has become another important aspect that is being incorporated in defining development. Sustainable development has been defined by the Brundtland Commission (1987, 43) as "development that meets the needs of present generation without compromising the ability of future generation to meet their own needs." Since 1992, Sustainable Human Development also became the official development paradigm of the UNDP. Sustainable development in mainstream thinking means little more than a mere environmentally conscious development.

As Goulet (1992, 496) has rightly pointed out, development is still operationally considered as the equivalent of "maximum economic growth and a drive towards industrialization and mass consumption." However, development, in these forms is not entirely sufficient. For instance, it has been observed that despite achieving striking economic and technological progress, in the United States, "uncertainties and anxieties are high, social and economic inequalities have widened considerably, social trust is on the decline, and confidence in the government is at all-time low." Economic prosperity in the United States failed to increase the self-reported happiness of its citizens (Sachs 2012, 3). It is observed (Thinley 1999,16) that ". . .beyond a level, an increase in material consumption is not accompanied by a concomitant rise in happiness". This becomes particularly prominent when development is measured in terms of increased human wellbeing instead of increased per capita income.

Thus, Bhutan has proposed and incorporated a concept of Gross National Happiness as the guiding philosophy of its development in place of indicators like the Gross Domestic Product (Hewavitharana 2004, 496–497). It proposes that the goal of development is to increase social happiness. Thus, the Bhutanese developmental approach consists of a set of policies that include: (1) economic self-reliance, (2) environmental preservation, (3) cultural promotion, and (4) good governance, aiming at enhancing the Gross National Happiness (Thinley 1999, 16).

Time and again, development has found various definitions. The concept of development has now come to incorporate factors such as changes in the society promoting economic growth, structural changes in terms of modernization, distributive growth, human development, sustainable development, and, most importantly, the collective happiness of the society. Thus, development is not merely an economic concept. The concept of development incorporates aspects that are economic as well as noneconomic in nature. To indicate the above-mentioned economic and noneconomic aspects of "development," we will use a term "social development."

1.3   Why Social Development Is Important?

Social development is one of the basic entitlements of all human beings. Thus, promoting social development has its own intrinsic value. Promotion of social development is also important for attaining economic development. For instance, if the members of a society are healthy and possess basic education, then that society is likely to be better placed for economic development due to the human resources enjoying better standards of living. At the same time, enhancing the surplus-generating capability of economic development with the help of healthy and better educated human resources will enable economic development to provide better funding for social development. Thus, social and economic development act complementary to each other (Sen 2003, 6–7).

1.4   Limited Affordability of the Government for Social Development

It is the responsibility of the government to fulfill the social and economic needs of all its citizens. Developed nations can fulfill the social and economic needs of their citizens to various degrees. However, the developing nations often fail to meet even the basic economic and social needs of the people. One important reason for this is that governments in developing countries often may not be able to meet the expenses of providing basic economic and social amenities to all its citizens. Non availability of funds in the government exchequer is often cited as a primary reason for the same. One solution for this problem is to find out ways to meet the social developmental needs of the people in a self-sustaining manner.

1.5   Business and Social Development

Beneficial Role of Profit-maximization Business

By business we commonly refer to what Muhammad Yunus has termed as "profit maximizing business" or which we may also refer to as "commercial business." Proponents of capitalist philosophy argue that the best solution for poverty is to allow business to flourish which by itself will solve the problem of poverty. The founding father of capitalism, Adam Smith (1937, 508; org.1776), for instance, argued that the individual pursuit of self-interest helps the entire society to prosper. From narrow self-interest comes, to use Smith's famous phrase, "greatest good of the greatest number of people." Thus, it may be argued that under an ideal capitalist economy, the problem of poverty will eventually be resolved through a commercial business model. Hence, the question of government playing a role in alleviating poverty does not arise.

We mention below some other arguments highlighting the poverty-alleviating role of the commercial business model. For instance, Brainard and LaFleur (2006, 1–28) in their article "The Private Sector in the Fight against Global Poverty" argued as follows on how the private sector can play a role in solving the problem of global poverty.

Firstly, they argue that by playing a very vital role in the development of the economy, the private sector provides income and employment to people. It makes goods and services available to people. "By generating jobs, serving the underserved, promoting innovation and spurring productivity, indigenous private sector development can raise living standards and promote opportunity."

Secondly, they argued that a free play of market forces and increased competition make goods and services cheaper, benefiting poor as well as the rich.

Thirdly, they point out that the private sector being the major source of tax revenue supports social services like healthcare and education.

Fourthly, it is argued that microenterprise improves the lives of the poorest members of the society and "can provide bottom-up growth and innovation, while large nationals and multinationals can link markets to broader, global opportunities."

Brainard and LaFleur (2006) further argue that to address the problem of global poverty what is required is empowering businesses to do business in the developing world. Here, the fundamental questions they ask are: "How can the climate be improved for private enterprise in developing countries?" "How can more private capital investment be channelled to poor countries?"

In fact, with the initiation of the economic reforms, developing countries are addressing these questions. There have been attempts by governments in developing countries to facilitate investment by the private sector and creating an environment so that private sector can flourish. Thus, there also has been competition among developing countries and among provincial governments within developing countries to attract foreign investment.

Critics of Profit Maximization Business

It may be pointed out here that the basic assumption of the above arguments is that capitalism is good for the society and, if capitalism flourishes, through economic process, ultimately, poverty will get eradicated. However, two points can be mentioned here. Firstly, why the need for introducing anti-poverty programs was felt? Anti-poverty programs were needed because the poor people failed to benefit from the process of development. This may be because the environment then was not very friendly to the private sector. What is the guarantee that a more private sector-friendly environment will ensure benefit to the poor? There is an apprehension, not without ground, that pro-capitalist reform may also cause greater disparity. Hence, the issue is how we ensure that the process of reform brings in prosperity and not accompanied by greater disparity. Secondly, it has been argued that to make the process of reform work, developing societies should first attain a minimum level of social development, which by facilitating economic development will enhance social development further. Countries that witnessed success from reforms also testify this (Sen 2003, 19–23). In sum, our argument is that some amount of poverty alleviation and social development should accompany the very process of expansion of the role of private sector. How can that be achieved? Following sections will address this question.

The main goal of a business is to earn profit by providing goods and services. Business normally aims at maximizing its profit. Obviously, to provide social development is not the primary concern of business. However, by providing goods and services, businesses generally provide very useful services to the society. But, as the main goal of business is profit maximization, for earning profit, at times, business operations may do harm to the society. For instance, for earning profits, a business may promote unnecessary or harmful consumption in society.

Social Development: Whose Responsibility?

To work for the social and economic development of the society, on the contrary, is the primary responsibility of the government. Besides the government, the NGOs also play a relatively limited role in promoting social development.

It may also be noted that among these three agencies – business, government, and NGO; business is usually the most efficient sector, in comparison with the government or NGO sectors. It is rather unfortunate that a relatively efficient sector such as the business is engaged in profit maximization and not in social development. Secondly, with the advent of liberalization, privatization, and globalization, the government is withdrawing from the social sector. Now the social sector would increasingly require fending for itself. Thus, there is the need for the social sector to become self-sustaining.

The most common way for funding social developmental needs of the people by the government is collecting tax from the people. In a developing country, often collected taxes may not be enough for meeting the required social developmental needs of the people. This happens for several reasons. Often people may not have enough income; hence, tax collection is poor. At times, the tax collection system may be defective – as a result, tax collection amount is poor due to large-scale tax evasion. Besides, often despite allotting tax payers' money for meeting social developmental needs, people fail to get the required services due to corruption and administrative inefficiency.

Often NGOs provide some social developmental services at a limited scale. For providing social developmental services NGOs depend on donation. However, due to limited availability of donations, such services are very limited in scope.

Under this situation, particularly in less-developed countries where state largely fails to meet social developmental needs due to lack of funds, one alternative way could be of meeting social developmental needs of the people by recovering the cost of providing these services from the recipient of those services. It should be noted that usually social developmental services are required to be provided to the poor. How can poor people pay for such services? This can be attempted, if such services are provided at a price affordable by the poor. Providing social developmental services to the poor at a price affordable by them would require some innovative steps. Can we think of a business which aims at not profit maximization, but providing social developmental services at a price affordable by the poor?

Types of Business Promoting Social Development

If we think of a business that aims at providing social developmental services to the poor at a price affordable by them and at least recover its cost that may be a solution. But for making that possible may involve not paying any dividend to its shareholders as is commonly done in the usual profit maximization business. Muhmmad Yunus has articulated one such business model which he calls "social business." Social business is one model through which social developmental services can be provided to the poor on a self-sustaining manner.

Further, there may be situations where social developmental services may be needed to be provided free of cost as poor people may not be able to pay for them. Besides, such a business also should make innovations in cost cutting and follow frugal entrepreneurial practices for making social developmental services affordable for the poor. In addressing such a situation, a unique business model of compassion has been developed by the Aravind Eye Care Hospital in Madurai, India. This hospital proactively provides free treatment to majority of its patients, but still it makes a profit. This has been made possible primarily through cross subsidy where cost of treating poor patients is met from the fees paid by the relatively richer patients who opt to pay for their treatment. How Aravind has done this will be discussed later.

Business is not poor-friendly, as a smaller capital or operation at a smaller scale, individually by the poor, makes it difficult for the poor to earn an income from business. To overcome this problem, a collective action by the poor by forming self-help groups and financing microenterprises through the mechanism of microcredit or forming of cooperative society also enables the poor to undertake income-generating activities and enhance their income. Thus, the mechanisms of self-help group and cooperatives also have helped the poor in their economic and social development.

C. K. Prahalad suggested a business model which he called "Bottom of the Pyramid" (BOP) business model. This model aims at marketing products and services to the "base of the income pyramid." It is argued that marketing goods and services to the poor by making them *affordable to the poor* enables a business to earn a profit; the same process also benefits the poor.

Also, there are examples of commercial business providing welfare services through business, which along with providing needed welfare service enables the poor to benefit from the operation of such a business.

Thus, there are several business models that make providing social developmental services in a self-sustaining manner possible without depending on any subsidy or donations. There are also forms of business operations that help the poor to increase their income. We will discuss these poor-friendly business models in the following chapters to examine their role in promoting social development.

An Alternative Viewpoint on the Role of Business in Society

There are two major positions about the role of business in society. The capitalist school holds that by allowing every individual to pursue their narrow self-interest through business will eventually create prosperity and alleviate poverty. The Marxist school, on the contrary, observes that in capitalist society, the capitalist class accumulates wealth by exploiting the working class through business. This results in inequality and poverty in the society. In this background, we propose a role of a business in society, which differs from both these positions. The goal of any business has been assumed as earning a profit. We, on the contrary, propose a business that aims at promoting social development and poverty alleviation. However, as it is a business, it must be self-sustaining or it must generate a surplus to survive. Thus, it is a business, but promotes social development. Some of the features of these business models are: it is "no loss, no dividend business," or it "cross-subsidizes services to the poor," or "profit goes to the poor" or it provides goods and services making it affordable for the poor. Benefiting the poor is the common goal of these business models.

According to Marx, in a capitalist society, the capitalist class or the owners of business make profit by exploiting the working class thus, causing poverty. Here, we are talking about a type of business, which will be so designed that they will be benefiting the poor. Saying so, we are contradicting what Marx said about the role of a business in a capitalist society. Our contention is that there are types of businesses that eradicate poverty and promote social development. Marx observed that in a capitalist society, profit earned in the business comes from "misappropriation" of surplus created by the workers. In the models of business that we will be discussing, the generated surplus primarily benefits the poor, through different arrangements. Thus, under these models of business, even if, we assume that there is exploitation of workers in the Marxian sense, the exploitation is compensated through generation of benefits to the poor. Marxists would be critical of these models of business by observing that in a capitalist society, the primary nature of business will remain exploitative and the so-called pro-poor business models will only create an illusion of better deals for the poor.

Thus, we argue that businesses aiming at only profit maximization are not the only form of businesses that exist. Of course, profit-maximizing business is the major form that we come across in capitalist societies. But, we argue that there are forms of businesses that aim at promoting social development too and help the poor to overcome poverty. We will discuss these poor-friendly business models in the following chapters.

CHAPTER 2

Social Business

Everywhere that societies exist there is altruism, because there is soliderity.

—**Durkheim** *The Division of Labour in Society*

2.1 What Is Social Business?

Nobel Laureate Muhammad Yunus has developed the concept of a new type of business, which he calls "Social Business" – a type of business that specifically aims at social development. Yunus pointed out that the present economic theory and the theory of capitalism assume that human beings are motivated only by self-interest. Thus, under these economic theories, it is assumed that human beings are only one-dimensional persons governed by narrow self-interest. Yunus argued that though most of the time human behavior is governed by self-interest, human beings also get engaged in serving the interest of the others. Otherwise, how is it that people make donations? The amount of donations made by people is not a small amount. The existence of a nonprofit sector of more than $1.1 trillion value (Salamon et al. 1999, 8) is an evidence of the same. The same person can work in self-interest for some time and may also work for other's interest at other times. For instance, Bill Gates was engaged in pursuing narrow economic self-interest so long as he was running his business. But when he created the Bill and Melinda Gates Foundation, he became engaged in serving others interest. Several examples of these types are present. Thus, Yunus pointed out that human beings are not one-dimensional, but multidimensional beings. He argues that if human beings are multidimensional, then there could be more than one type of business. One is the type of business we commonly see, the profit maximizing business, where the goal of the business is to maximize profits for the self. He observes that there could be another type of business where the goal is to serve the interest of others, and not of the self alone. He calls this business as "social business." Unlike "profit maximizing business," the goal of a social business is to serve a social cause. It aims at providing goods and services to the poor at a price affordable to them. Alongside, services and goods are offered at a price so that at least the cost is recovered, to keep the business self-sustaining. Social business cannot make loss indefinitely. Because if it runs at a loss, then it cannot be self-sustaining. The business will be eventually closed and will not be able to serve the social purpose for which it was set-up. On the contrary, when the business makes a profit it does not give any dividend to any individual; any profit earned in social business is ploughed back into the business to serve the interests of the people better. Yunus (2008, xvi) observes that social business is "a business designed to meet a social goal . . . A social business is a business that pays no dividends. It sells products at prices that make it self-sustaining. The owners of the company can get back the amount they've invested in the company over a period of time, but no profit is paid to investors in the form of dividends. Instead, any profit made stays in the business—for finance expansion, to create new products or services, and to do more good for the world." Thus, according to Yunus (2008, 24), the social business is a *"non-loss, non-dividend business."*

Few questions may be raised about the feasibility of the above concept of a social business, particularly from the viewpoint of one-dimensional human beings who are concerned only with economic interest for the self. Firstly, if a social business does not give any dividend, persons interested only in narrow self-interest will not be interested in investing in the social business. Based on his concept of multidimensional human beings, Yunus has argued that those who donate for charity will be more interested in giving their money for social business. Charity money as such has only one life. It gets exhausted serving the purpose of charity. But, in social business, money gets many lives as the money comes back and gets re-invests. Thus, it can have a much greater impact than money given for charity. Thus, social businesses can be initiated by collecting donations. Those who want to involve themselves for solving some social problem will not hesitate to donate money for social businesses, Yunus argued.

Yunus has suggested that a social business can get its capital by taking long-term loans at a lower interest from generosity-minded people. The loan amount can be returned once the business becomes viable. Yunus has identified following seven types of sources of investment for social business: (1) existing companies; (2) foundations; (3) individual successful entrepreneurs; (4) international donor agencies; (5) governments; (6) retired persons; and (7) young people.

We feel that there is an issue regarding motivation behind running a social business. In a profit maximizing business, earning profit works as a driving force of the business. A social business is devoid of that motivation as in social business, any profit earned does not go to any individual, but is reinvested in the business. Thus, a social business may lack a zeal for earning profit, which may adversely affect its operation and hinder it from becoming a successful, viable business. On the contrary, a charity-based nongovernmental organization (NGO) is driven by a motivation to serve people. One may wonder, being devoid of both profit incentives of a profit maximization business and the service motive of a philanthropy-based NGO, what will work as the motivating force of a social business? The present author was involved in a social business experiment, which he studied as a participant observer. The present author had an opportunity to closely observe the shaping of that social business experiment, which has been narrated under section 2.3. The pleasant discovery of that social business experiment is that *the zeal to serve a social purpose in a self-reliant manner* became the driving force and the most-important contributing factor in the success of that social business. This confirmed Yunus's observation that replacing greed, serving social goals can be a powerful motivational force for running a free enterprise (Yunus 2007, 215). Thus, whereas the value base of a charity-based NGO is to provide services to others, earning profit is the value base of a profit maximizing business. The value base of a social business is serving a social cause through self-reliance.

2.2   Scope of a Social Business

One important aspect of a social business is that it is a self-sustaining way of promoting social development. This is an important aspect of the concept of social business, particularly, when under the influence of neo-liberal philosophy, the state is increasingly withdrawing from its social developmental role. When the state withdraws from providing for social development, the role of social business to promote social development in a self-sustaining manner becomes significant.

Secondly, particularly the developing countries where social problems are widespread, the government often fails to meet the social developmental needs of the people. There are several reasons for the same. One major source of funds for meeting the social developmental needs of the people is to collect tax. Often less-developed economies may have limited scope to collect tax due to limited earnings. Yunus observed (2010, 23) "Government uses taxpayer money in its attempts to solve social problems, and therefore it is limited by resource base. Social business, by contrast, can be expanded indefinitely by raising investment money from every imaginable source".

Thirdly, at times, inefficient tax collection system often results in limited fund in the government exchequer, adversely affecting spending for social development.

Fourthly, even the allocated amount for social development is often spent inefficiently or inappropriately. For instance, referring to misappropriation of welfare funds, Rajiv Gandhi, the then prime minister of India once observed that every rupee spent by the government for social welfare, only 15 paisa (which is around one-seventh of the fund allocated) reached the intended beneficiary. The situation holds true even today.[1] Thus, Yunus (2007, 214) argued that government should withdraw from promoting social development. Instead social businesses – "a social consciousness-driven private sector" should promote social development.

We, however, feel that though social business may be an efficient alternative in promoting social development, the government should have the primary responsibility to meet the social needs of the people. Also, the government should promote social business in fulfilling social goals, where needed. Besides, charity will always have its role in society. For instance, when natural disasters like flood or earthquake destroys normal life, reaching out and helping people are essential. Also, there are some categories of people who must rely on charity for survival. For instance, people who suffer from extreme physical or mental disabilities or those who are very old would require support from charity. Thus, Yunus (2010, 6–7) observed ". . .not all charity should be replaced by social business. Sometimes simply helping people in desperate need is essential . . .there is room in our world for charity, just there is room for social business".

There are so many social problems and hardships faced by poor people. For instance, there are problems of poverty, health, education, etc. One can think of business ideas to solve those problems in a self-sustaining manner through social business. Social business is a good example of how social development can be achieved in self-sustaining manner through business.

To explain the concept of social business further and how social business can promote social development, in the section that follows, we have discussed how an NGO moved from philanthropic mode to self-sustaining mode by setting up a social business to mitigate the problem of child malnutrition. It also shows the type of hurdles faced by an NGO in moving from philanthropy to a self-sustaining mode. Learning about this journey may be useful for an NGO. This recounting draws upon the author's observation of this process as a participant observer.

2.3   Making of a Social Business: Toward a Self-reliant Way of Achieving Social Development

In the post liberalization era, with the gradual withdrawal of government from social development, availability of government funds for social development became limited. At the same time, particularly in countries like India, NGOs are finding it difficult to attract foreign funding as post liberalized India with high growth rate is not considered among the least developed countries that normally attract international aid and donation. Thus, due to the want of government funding and international donations, there is a need to think of alternative ways of funding social development. Besides, there are viewpoints that decry dependence on charity and propagate self-reliant ways of promoting social development (Yunus 2008). Dees (1998, 2012), Sriram (2011), Yunus (2008), Mehta and Shenoy (2012), among others have discussed the issues relating to two different approaches – charity and self-reliance, in addressing social problems. They have highlighted the contribution of the approach based on business methods and self-reliance in solving social problems. It is under this background that we examine how one charity-based NGO in India is moving progressively toward self-reliance in some of its activities through social business. The recounting is based on participant observation of this process by the present author. Here, an attempt has been made to draw lessons from this process in moving toward self-reliance in achieving social development.

The account is organized as follows. The section "Child in Need Institute (CINI)" gives a brief introduction about the NGO, Child in Need Institute (CINI), which has initiated this process of self-reliance. The section "CINI's Work in Developing and Distributing Supplementary Infant Food to Mitigate Child Malnutrition" narrates the work of this NGO in mitigating child malnutrition by developing and promoting the use of a low-cost supplementary food among the needy. The section "CINI Nutrimix Social Business (CNSB)" discusses how a gradual shifting of this charity-based work toward self-reliance took shape primarily through social business and, finally, the section "Discussion and Concluding Observations" draws lessons from this process and makes concluding observations.

Child in Need Institute (CINI)

In the early 1970s, Dr. Samir Narayan Chaudhuri, an ex-army doctor having specialized in pediatrics started a clinic, in association with Christian missionaries, to provide free treatment to malnourished children among the poor in the fringe of Kolkata (then known as Calcutta). Soon, he realized that there is no simple clinical solution to the problem of malnutrition, which has its roots in some other ailments in the society. He wondered how to overcome those problems. Ultimately, the quest for a solution to the problem of child malnutrition transformed this doctor into a social worker who, eventually set up an NGO, the Child in Need Institute (CINI) in 1974, to fight the problem of child malnutrition and other associated social problems.

Presently, CINI primarily operates in the states of West Bengal, Jharkhand, and Chhattisgarh in India. The CINI's mission and vision is "Sustainable development in health, nutrition, education and protection of child, adolescent and women in need." The exemplary work of CINI spreading over period more than four decades has received wide recognition both in India and internationally. The CINI and Dr. Chaudhuri have received several awards. For instance, CINI received the prestigious National Award for Child Welfare by the Government of India twice, in 1985 and 2004. In 2011, CINI received the WHO Award for Excellence in Primary Health Care. The award list is long.

Details about CINI's activities and achievements are available in its website (http://www.cini-india.org/).

In 1974, CINI was set up as a charity-based organization. During its long journey, CINI's strategy of operation evolved, depending on its experience and learning from prevailing situations. However, all along, CINI remained a predominantly philanthropy-based organization. Two major sources of funds for CINI have been grants from the government for undertaking various social developmental activities and donations from multinational organizations and fund-raising outfits of CINI, located in some developed countries. The remaining funding came through CINI's local fund-raising activities. Post 1990, as India entered the liberalization era, CINI faced considerable resource crunch due to the developments mentioned earlier. Thus, running this organization entirely based on donations was becoming increasingly difficult. It is under this backdrop that Dr. Chaudhuri and CINI's board members increasingly felt the need of moving from charity toward self-reliance in some of its activities. This was a significant paradigm shift for a philanthropy-based organization. Here, I will try to capture how this paradigm shift was initiated and how it took shape. This became a significant move because, as we will see later, this move not only enabled CINI to make a greater impact in removing child malnutrition by making production and distribution of low-cost supplementary infant food more efficient, widespread and self-reliant, it also provided funding support to CINI, in its other activities also.

CINI's Work in Developing and Distributing Supplementary Infant Food to Mitigate Child Malnutrition

Given the remarkable economic growth over the last decade, it often becomes difficult to believe that India ranked 100th position among 119 countries on Global Hunger Index 2017. According to 2015–2016 survey data, 'more than a fifth (21 percent) children in India suffer from wasting . . . Further, India's child wasting rate has not substantially improved over the last 25 years . . . Its child stunting rate . . . still relatively high at 38.4 percent' (Grember et al. 2017, 12). The stunted physical and cognitive development caused by malnutrition last a lifetime and the associated economic losses are estimated at 3 percent of India's GDP annually (Nandi Foundation 2011, 8). Thus, for the betterment of health, education, and economic development of the country, the need for eradicating malnutrition cannot be overemphasized. The CINI, on its part, is making very valuable contribution in fighting malnutrition and some other ailments for more than four decades now. Here, we will restrict our focus on a small part of CINI's work – its work relating to promotion of a nutritious supplementary infant food in mitigating child malnutrition.

CINI's Innovation in Mitigating Child Malnutrition

The CINI is working to prevent and overcome malnourishment of children among the poor since its inception in 1974. Through its work among the malnourished children, doctors in CINI working under the leadership of Dr. Chaudhuri identified one important cause of child malnutrition among the families of the poor as follows. For the first 6 months after birth, a breastfed child gets all nutritional requirements from breast milk. After that age, along with breast milk, children must also be given high-quality, nutrient-rich foods. That is not a problem for the children in developed counties and children of the rich and middle class in developing countries. Those children are given various nutrition-rich baby foods mainly marketed by multinational companies. However, poor families cannot afford those baby foods as they are very expensive for them. The type of food they give to the children often lack in the required nutrients. The doctors in CINI, based on their work at the grassroots – in the villages and urban slums, identified this as a compelling cause of malnutrition among the children of the poor families. Thus, they felt the need for developing a low-cost, nutrition-rich, supplementary food for the children of the poor families. Identification of this problem and its above-mentioned remedy may appear to be common knowledge today. But, this was not so way back in 1974, when CINI started its work on this. The CINI was a pioneer in developing a low-cost, nutritious supplementary infant food named as Nutrimix. For developing this food, Dr. Chaudhuri consulted an expert, the then Head of the Department of Food Technology at the Jadavpur University, Calcutta, Professor Sunit Mukherjee. This coming together of these two persons with a strong passion for a social cause, of a medical doctor turned social worker and a renowned scientist,[2] was a defining moment for CINI's work. Dr. Chaudhuri saw in Prof. Mukherjee a person who could be guiding force for CINI's work, particularly in fighting malnutrition and fruitfully persuaded Prof. Mukherjee to join CINI's Board as its President. This association is continuing from that time till date.

Thus, due to unavailability of a low-cost weaning food for young children, a low-cost food has been developed by CINI way back in 1970s. This food had undergone several tests at the Nutrition Rehabilitation Centre run by CINI and at Prof. Sunit Mukherjee's laboratory with encouraging results. Developing Nutrimix was a successful innovation of CINI in tackling child malnutrition among the poor. Below we will describe how Nutrimix was promoted by CINI for mitigating malnutrition. The significance of CINI's work in developing a low cost supplementary food like Nutrimix and its promotion is obvious in the following observation about India in the report of 2017 Global Hunger Index (Grember et al. 2017, 12). It observes, "Areas of concern include 1) the timely introduction of complementary food for young children (that is, the transition away from exclusive breast feeding), which declined from 52.7 percent to 42.6 percent between 2006 and 2016; 2) the share of children between 6 and 23 months old who receive an adequate diet- a mere 9.6 for the country; . . ."

As we will see below, the production and promotion of Nutrimix have gone through some stages.

Evolution of Nutrimix

Free Distribution of Nutrimix (1974 to 1978). The CINI has a clinic in the campus of its Head Office, located at Pailan, 24 Parganas (South), West Bengal. Pregnant and lactating mothers and children up to the age of five, from among the poor families were provided free medical checkup and remedial services. As often visiting children at this clinic were found to be malnourished, as a part of remedial service, CINI used to make Nutrimix manually and used to cook it to feed those children. Visiting mothers were also given a packet of Nutrimix and were instructed on how to cook the same at home for feeding the child. Being a philanthropy-based organization providing service to the needy, mothers were provided a packet of Nutrimix almost free of cost. A nominal amount of just Rs 2/-

was collected for a packet of 500 grams of Nutrimix. The emphasis was in building awareness in the community about giving the child this low-cost weaning food. It was thought that the children of the poor families could be effectively helped to come out of malnutrition thus.

One limitation of this service was that the mother could collect Nutrimix almost free of cost only on visiting CINI's clinic. As often the mothers used to come from far off villages and not having effective communication systems, visiting CINI's clinic just to collect a packet of Nutrimix was not always easy. Another limitation of this act of giving Nutrimix free of cost was that at times value of Nutrimix for meeting the nutritional requirement of the child was not realized and it was reported in a survey that there were instances where the poor households used Nutrimix as fodder, instead of feeding the child. Not very surprising in a country where ignorance and poverty are so widespread. And of course, free distribution of Nutrimix was dependent on donation.

Community-centric Manual Production and Distribution (1979 to 2009). Being aware of the above limitations of solely donation-based free distribution of Nutrimix; for a wider and self-reliant promotion of Nutrimix, CINI decided to teach mothers how to prepare Nutrimix at home for feeding the child. Free distribution of Nutrimix from CINI's clinic continued, but for a wider spread of the benefit of Nutrimix, CINI organized camps at its mobile clinics and at villages where social workers from CINI taught mothers how to make Nutrimix at home. This well-thought out strategy was a significant step by CINI, from charity toward self-reliance. This step aiming at sustainability almost echoed the famous proverb "Give a man a fish; you have fed him for today. Teach a man to fish; and you have fed him for a lifetime".

Limited Spread of Nutrimix.   For more than three decades, free distribution of Nutrimix and teaching mothers to prepare Nutrimix at home were the two main ways of spreading the use of Nutrimix followed by CINI. The CINI could have felt satisfied with its achievements in developing Nutrimix and promoting its use as described above, and could have happily lived on its laurels. However, being an organization constantly trying to excel and innovate, it was felt by Dr. Chaudhuri and CINI's board members that given the enormous potentiality of Nutrimix to contribute in checking child malnutrition and given the widespread suffering of the children in India from malnutrition, Nutrimix could do better. It was felt that the use of Nutrimix did not spread enough. Not many people knew about it, despite its long existence. Reasons were obvious. Firstly, the knowledge about Nutrimix and its benefits remained confined only among those mothers who encountered CINI. Secondly, often the overworked mothers of low-income families found preparation of Nutrimix involving roasting, grinding, and mixing of the ingredients in right quantity, cumbersome and time consuming, and were not always able to find time for that. Thirdly, given their living condition, some of the low-income households were not in a favorable position to prepare Nutrimix properly or hygienically. Fourthly, it was felt that if the preparation of Nutrimix is mechanized and if it is produced in large quantity; providing economy of scale, it would be more cost effective and would be of improved quality due to mechanized production than mothers preparing Nutrimix at home in small quantities. Should the poor households remain deprived of this cost-effective option of benefiting from Nutrimix? Above all, free distribution of Nutrimix depending on donation, suffered from fund shortages. These factors led to the idea of spreading the use of Nutrimix in a self-reliant way through a new concept of "social business." In the section that follows, we will discuss how this idea took shape.

CINI Nutrimix Social Business (CNSB)

The Initiation (2009 to 2011)

Muhmmad Yunus published his book "Creating a World without Poverty: Social Business and the Future of Capitalism" in 2008 where he articulated the concept of "social business." On learning about this concept of "'social business," Dr. Chaudhuri and some other board members of CINI were contemplating with the idea of setting up a social business of Nutrimix for spreading the benefits of Nutrimix in self-reliant manner for mitigating child malnutrition.

However, being a charity-based organization with no experience and expertise in business, this appeared to be a wishful thinking. Besides, the initial capital for such a venture was not readily available. There was also a strong hesitation among the old timers in CINI, groomed under the philanthropy school of providing free service to people, to go for business. That it would not be a "profit maximizing business" but a "social business" did not hold much water. Dees' (2012) observation that "Nonprofit . . .just not accustomed to the idea that good might be done (even more) effectively through market-based approaches, leveraging charitable contributions with earned income" is pertinent here.

There was a small solace on the lack of expertise in business type activity in CINI. In an informal way, CINI developed a close relationship with a reputed business school, the Indian Institute of Management Calcutta (IIMC). This informal association benefited both organizations. The IIMC students often approached CINI either to work on a project assigned to them as a part of a course work at IIMC or as a student intern or undertaking an assignment for CINI as a part of a service to CINI. The CINI being an organization working in close contact with the community provided an excellent learning opportunity for the students about grassroots level reality. The CINI also welcomed student interns from IIMC. Apart from this type of association, another important form of CINI–IIMC association was that some IIMC faculty members served as members of CINI's Governing Board. Below, we will narrate the CINI–IIMC interaction around Nutrimix.

The present author as a faculty member of IIMC then, introduced the concept of "social business" in one of his courses that he taught at IIMC. This course involved project work on the topics taught in the class. Thus, as a topic for the project work, it was suggested to a group of students to develop a business plan for CINI's Nutrimix, following the concept of social business that was discussed in the class. On completion of the project work, students were required to make a presentation in the class on their project report. This project work being related to CINI, Dr. Chaudhuri was invited to be present in the class at IIMC at the time of the presentation of this report. He obliged and came with two of his senior colleagues for that presentation and gave his feedback. A copy of this project report (Beejal et al. 2008) was also presented to him. Those project reports were limited in scope, prepared within the time limit of a class assignment. The purposes of those exercises were for creating an opportunity for the students for practical application of the concepts discussed in the class. In the case of this project report, it was also thought that this exercise may facilitate thinking in CINI in proceeding for Nutrimix social business.

However, the one important hindrance for going ahead with the social business of Nutrimix was unavailability of a fund to set it up. It was thought that deploying a fund by CINI for this social business will be risky, particularly, in view of the lack of expertise in taking up such an endeavor. Fortunately, an opportunity to explore this idea of social business came through a World Bank sponsored event. World Bank had announced an award grant competition – "South Asia Regional Development Marketplace 2009. Innovate for Nutrition" (http://web .worldbank.org/WBSITE/EXTERNAL/COUNTRIES/SOUTHASIAE XT/0,,contentMDK:22041113~pagePK:146736~piPK:146830~theSit ePK:223547,00.html), inviting innovative proposals for reducing child malnutrition in South Asia. Dr. Chaudhuri brought this announcement to my notice and suggested that as my students have done some preliminary work in preparing a business plan for Nutrimix social business, I should take the initiative to prepare a proposal around that idea as an innovative proposal for reducing child malnutrition for this award grant competition. The announcement mentioned that NGOs can collaborate with educational institutions in participating in this competition. I agreed to take the initiative and it was decided that it will be proposed that CINI will be the implementing agency of this proposal and we from IIMC will collaborate (informally) with CINI in developing the proposal and be involved in advisory capacity.

One of my PhD students with a background in nutrition agreed to work for developing the proposal. The CINI also deputed one of its employees having relevant expertise to work for the proposal. We prepared the proposal for submission in this competition. In brief, we proposed to undertake a "social business" of Nutrimix, involving mechanized production of Nutrimix to be marketed by self-help groups of women targeting "the bottom of the pyramid market" (Prahalad 2005). Following the norm of social business, the goal of this social business would be to promote the use of Nutrimix by selling it at a price affordable for the poor, at the same time at least recovering the cost and, thereby, serving the cause of removing malnutrition in a self-reliant manner by promoting effective use of Nutrimix. As per the norm of social business, any profit earned will not go to any individual, but will be ploughed back in this business (Yunus 2008, 24), for removing malnutrition more extensively. It was felt that in this way, it would be possible also to overcome the problem of limited spread of Nutrimix through extended marketing and widen the impact of Nutrimix in removal of child malnutrition.

Our proposal was shortlisted in the first stage of screening (http://siteresources.worldbank.org/SOUTHASIAEXT/Resources /223546-1171488994713/3455847-1232124140958/5748939 -1234285802791/SARDM2009Finalists.pdf). Thus, we were invited to Dhaka, Bangladesh to showcase and explain our proposal to an international jury of experts. My PhD student who was involved in developing the proposal was deputed to go to Dhaka for this purpose. Fortunately, our proposal was shortlisted among the 21 prize-winning proposals and CINI was awarded $40,000 to implement this project over a period of 18 months. The CINI was required to implement this project with this World Bank award grant adding its own contributions.

Thus, CINI Nutrimix Social Business (CNSB) came into being. The plant was set up at the campus of CINI's headoffice located at Pailan near Kolkata. This plant was inaugurated on 29th April 2010, when mechanized production of Nutrimix started in this plant. Thus, more than three decades of manual production of Nutrimix came to an end and Nutrimix entered into the era of mechanized production and social business mode.

The Period of "Teething Trouble" and Creative Excitement

Limitation of Human Resources.   The first step in setting up CNSB was to recruit a person who would oversee the day-to-day operation of this social business. Thus, the post was advertised, and a person was selected for the post of Manager, CNSB, through a selection interview. Within the limit of the available fund, the salary that could be offered to the CNSB Manager was not commensurate enough to recruit a professional for this position. Thus, a science graduate with some relevant work experience was recruited for the post. Organizationally CNSB was placed under the Division of Child Health and Development (DCHD) at the CINI's head office. The Manager, CNSB was to report to the Assistant Director, DCHD – who was a medical doctor. Point to be noted here is that setting up CINI Nutrimix Social Business and the execution of the initial business activities were done, not by any professionally trained person in business or a person having experience in business, but by a novice Manager of CNSB under the supervision of a medical doctor.

Setting Up of the Factory.   It was decided to set up the factory in the campus of the head office of CINI at Pailan, in the South 24 Parganas district, West Bengal, India. The factory was set up by vacating a godown space in the premises of the CINI head office. Thus, no additional cost was required for construction of the factory premise, apart from the renovation cost of the godown for setting up the factory. The first task of the newly appointed Manager was to purchase the required machineries for the factory. Neither the Manager nor his supervisor – a medical doctor, had any previous experience or knowledge regarding machineries to be bought for this factory. Fortunately, Prof Sunit Mukherjee, the President of CINI, is an expert in this area. In this matter, apart from theoretical knowledge about the machineries, one should also have practical knowledge and experience regarding suppliers of those machines, their credentials, quality of after-sales service etc. Fortunately, Prof. Mukherjee had vast knowledge in both aspects as he regularly dealt with those types of machines and their suppliers in his laboratories. Thus, under the very able guidance of Prof. Mukherjee, the machineries were procured for the Nutrimix factory. However, due to limited availability of funds, and due to time constraints of this time-bound project, at times compromises had to be made in procuring of right type of machineries. As a result, later production processes were often hampered due to inefficient functioning and occasional breakdown of machines.

Venturing into Business Activity in a Charitable Organization. Undertaking business type activity in a charitable organization was the biggest challenge faced by CNSB. Old timers in CINI, who were also enjoying more power, did not like the idea of CINI getting into business type activities. This is natural to expect in an organization where providing service to others (free of cost) based on philanthropy remained the norm. Depriving this philanthropy-based organization from the noble feeling of "service" and "giving" by setting up CNSB may have given a feeling to some of its old timers of a paradise lost. Thus, at the inception, the CNSB was like an unwanted imposition for old timers of CINI. They were also the powerful sections among CINI's staff. The founder of CINI, Dr. Chaudhuri often being away for raising fund for CINI, these old timers were deputed to look after the day-to-day activities of CINI and thus, took most of the operational decisions. I will present some instances of hindrances faced by CNSB from this powerful section of CINI's staff. This in no way a depiction of weakness of this philanthropy-based organization, but aims at giving a glimpse of the hindrances this type of business-oriented transformation of a philanthropy-based organization may have to face.

Dees (2012) observed, "according to the culture of charity, giving is superior". Such a feeling existed in CINI. For instance, one senior Assistant Director told the CNSB Manager "You stretch your hand for taking from the people (referring to the move from free distribution of Nutrimix to charging a price for Nutrimix), but we are here to give people (implying, hence we – the parsons involved in charity – are superior)". But ironically, this person did not realize that the CNSB was set up with a goal to reduce CINI's dependence on charity money.

In fact, the culture of charity and attempts to become self-reliant remained two distinct modes of helping people. "They can work hand-in-hand or they can be at odds." Let me point out some of the "odds" observed between these two cultures in CINI.

The Manager of CNSB was not welcomed by a section of employees of CINI, particularly by the powerful old timers from the very beginning. The reason being while others were engaged in charity-related activities, this new person would be engaged in "business," which was perceived as demeaning activity by the old timers.

Fortunately, the Manager who was appointed in CNSB was highly motivated in his work. That he was working very hard and demonstrating his competence by showing something concrete in terms of setting up the production unit of Nutrimix, was not liked by those who enjoyed a powerful position within CINI. They felt threatened that their superior position might get challenged by the performance shown by this new entrant.

A place was identified for locating the CNSB's production unit. That place was used as a storage place of old papers and some other junk items. Making this place available for setting up the production unit of CNSB was required. This required administrative action on the part of the respective administrative head, who also enjoyed a position of power in CINI. The manager of the CNSB did not enjoy his cooperation in making that place available by vacating it. This was delaying the process of going ahead and the work for setting up the plant was getting delayed. Subsequently, under pressure from many quarters, when he had to act in vacating that place, there was a sudden unusual outburst from him for being pressurized to make way for setting up of the production unit of CNSB. This incident indirectly reflected his frustration toward some developments he did not want to take place.

When the production unit was ready, it was needed to put up a signboard outside the production unit. It was decided that the signboard should carry the name as "CINI Nutrimix Social Business" in English. It was thought that the name should also be written in the local language, Bengali, keeping in mind its clientele. In literal Bengali translation, the option was to call it as "CINI Nutrimix *Samajik Byabsa*" (literal Bengali translation of "social business"). It was also found out that the literal translation of "Social Business" as "*samajik byabsa*" is commonly used in Bangladesh (a Bengali-speaking country like West Bengal), where many social businesses were in operation. However, it was felt unanimously by the senior officials in CINI, that the Bengali word for "business" – "*byabsa*" should not be used. For a charity-based NGO like CINI, "*byabsa*" or "business" was a "demeaning" ward, and that some other term having the same meaning should be used. Thus, it was decided that instead of "*byabsa*" or "business," another Bengali term with a similar meaning – "*udyoug*" or "enterprise" should be used. Thus, CNSB production unit signboard carried its name in English as "CINI Nutrimix Social Business" and, in Bengali, it was written as "CINI Nutrimix *Samajik Udyoug.*" There was absolutely nothing wrong in this Bengali translation of the word "social business" as "*samajik udyog,*" rather it sounds well, infusing a sense of entrepreneurship. But what is of interest is that this small incident illustrated the aversion to the idea of "business" in a charity-based organization like CINI.

The CNSB Manager's residence was located at a far-off place from his office. He had to commute a long distance to come to work and he was never late in reporting to office. As commuting was taking too much of his time and was tiring, he thought of staying near CINI and would go home during the weekends and holidays. He thought that would give him more time for work, which he needed at this initial stage of setting up of the plant and business. The CINI had some single-occupancy accommodations vacant in the premises of its head office where the Nutrimix manufacturing unit was located. He approached the administrative authority to allot him one such accommodation to facilitate his work. His request was not granted despite a vacant accommodation being available. This was a demonstration of another resistance from the powerful old-timers. The Manager, CNSB, then rented an accommodation near CINI head office and started staying there though that meant paying a good amount from his meager salary and also staying away from home. On learning about this, for facilitating the work of the Manager CNSB, one member of the CINI's Governing Board intervened and the CNSB Manager was ultimately provided accommodation inside CINI campus.

We have presented instances of some hindrances faced by the CNSB particularly at the initial stage. We feel that this was nothing, but a demonstration of conflict between two diverse cultures, the culture of charity and the culture of self-reliance.

Innovations and Product Improvement.   When Nutrimix was distributed free, it was packaged in a packet of 500 grams. When it was decided that Nutrimix will be sold, a point came up for consideration as to in what quantity packets and price Nutrimix should be sold. It was pointed out that as Nutrimix will be sold targeting the "bottom of the pyramid" market, reality of that market segment should be kept in mind in deciding about the packaging and pricing of Nutrimix.

Accordingly, it was decided to sell Nutrimix in sachets of 20 grams, the recommended per feed quantity for a child. One such packet was priced Rs 2, three such packets together – the recommended per day intake of Nutrimix for a child, was priced at Rs 5/-. Packaging in this quantity and the price assigned were thought suitable for making Nutrimix affordable to the "bottom of the pyramid" market segment. It was found out that such a pricing would be affordable to the poor. Thus, it was decided that the price had to be kept fixed at that for keeping it affordable to the poor households and at least the production cost, if not more, had to be recovered at that price. That was a challenge.

Secondly, the packaging was done keeping in mind the shelf life and storing and usage convenience of the poor households. Besides, this type of packaging would also facilitate consumption of Nutrimix in right quantity. It would also facilitate a hygienic way of using Nutrimix, as Nutrimix could be poured directly to a container from the sachet for preparing it for feeding the child, avoiding any likely contamination due to the use of any unclean medium (hand or spoon) while preparing Nutrimix.

The problem of storage of Nutrimix by the poor families was also considered. Nutrimix was packed keeping in mind the living condition of the very poor families. For instance, families living in urban slums, or migrant laborers families living at the temporary work sites also would be able to safely store such Nutrimix sachets avoiding contamination.

Being a "social business," the goal of the CNSB was to facilitate effective use of Nutrimix in preventing malnutrition. The above type of packaging was thought of keeping those concerns in mind. The packaging material was selected accordingly and the automated airtight packaging machine was thus, designed. This type of packaging and pricing, keeping the living condition of the people at the base of the income pyramid in mind, was an important innovation of CNSB. If this was just a profit maximizing business, emphasis would have been more on amount sold with profit and not that much on its effective end use.

However, it should be noted that above innovations in packaging were relevant as long as the strategy was to sell Nutrimix through self-help groups directly to the poorer households to be used by the family members to feed the children. But, as we have mentioned later under the section CINCOMM, the strategy of selling Nutrimix shifted to bulk sell to the Integrated Child Development Services (ICDS) program. As under the ICDS program, children were feed Nutrimix at the ICDS center (*Anganbari*) by the *Anganbari* teacher by preparing it in bulk, it was assumed that they will follow the hygienic practices in storing and preparing Nutrimix. It was felt that packaging Nutrimix in packets of half kilogram with suitable packaging material will be appropriate. Thus, to the ICDS, Nutrimix is given in half kilogram packets with appropriate packaging material. Innovations are situation specific.

Some other measures such as improved hygienic practices for the workers and other staff members were introduced like: workers were required to put on headcover and hand gloves, and remove shoes used by them outside and put on separate clean shoes kept for using only within the factory premises. Outside visitors also required to adhere to the above types of norms for visiting factory premises etc.

When something is sold for a price, instead of distributing it free to its users, "they become customers, empowered to complain, instead of being passive, grateful recipients of charity." Such developments happened for Nutrimix. For instance, there was a complaint from the customers that children did not like its taste. During more than three decades of existence of Nutrimix, no such complaint was made. Probably, the recipient of free Nutrimix thought that as they were getting it free, they should not complain about its taste etc.

Nutrimix was distributed as a *ready-to-cook* food for the child. That meant mothers need to cook Nutrimix for a little while before giving it to the child. Some mothers said that they prefer a food for the child which is *ready to eat* for the child like some other baby foods available in the market. They find ready-to-eat food as convenient because it is not time consuming in cooking.

In response to these types of feedbacks from customers, sugar and organic flavors were added to make Nutrimix tasty. Nutrimix was made *ready to eat* (rather than *ready to cook*) by making it more roasted. That also added to its shelf life. Further, it was decided to improve the quality of Nutrimix by fortifying it with iodine and iron, the deficiencies from which the children of its target group often suffer.

Thus, selling of Nutrimix made its customers asking for better quality and convenience, comparing it with other products in the market. This process contributed in improving the product. It also resulted a packaging that facilitated its consumption in the right quantity hygienically and brought storing convenience. Nutrimix, as a product, had remained the same throughout its existence over a period of more than three decades as in its free distribution, there was no compulsion in improving its quality. Recipients were grateful that they were getting Nutrimix free and, on the part of CINI also, naturally no urge was felt to put in extra efforts and investments on something which was distributed free. Interestingly, within a brief period of entering the social business mode, product development became an integral concern in producing Nutrimix. This is only natural to expect. As soon as a price is charged for a product, the quality of the product comes under scrutiny, more so in a competitive market. Yunus (2008, 27) has rightly observed that social business "brings the advantage of free-market competition into the world of social improvement".

Continuation of CNSB beyond World Bank-assisted Initiation

The primary goal of a social business is to serve a social cause and not profit maximization. This should not give the impression that making profit is of less importance in a social business. If a social business runs at a loss indefinitely, its very existence will be threatened and if it fails to maintain financial viability, it would be closed and thus, will fail to serve the social cause it intended to serve. Thus, though the primary goal of social business is to serve a social cause, social businesses must also make profit so that they can survive without depending on any subsidy. Thus, it is important to look at the financial performance of CNSB.

By the end of 18 months of its operation under the sponsorship of World Bank, the CNSB was left with a surplus of Rs 4,90,520/- ($7,623)[3] in its kitty as well as the factory with all its machineries, trained manpower, and the rich experience and learning from running the business for 18 months. Of course, when we discount the World Bank grant from this, CNSB did not make any profit in the real sense during the first 18 months of its operation. But, looking at the trend of income of the first 18 months, neither could we conclude that CNSB would not be a sustainable and viable social business. The 18-month period's experience was too short to arrive at such conclusion. This 18-month period also was the difficult "teething trouble" period of CNSB.

Marketing of Nutrimix remained as one key area of challenge. The CNSB proposed to sell Nutrimix through self-help groups of women and thus, also aimed at economic empowerment of women. It was proposed that CNSB would undertake promotional activities for Nutrimix by organizing health camps in the villages. However, that could not be undertaken to the extent required due to lack of manpower. The CNSB manager was so pre-occupied with work at the factory and office that he could devote very little time to visit villages for the promotion of Nutrimix. Thus, there was very limited information dissemination about Nutrimix, which affected the sale of Nutrimix adversely. Based on the experience of these 18 months of gestation period of CNSB, it was felt that with improved managerial support, CNSB possessed the potentiality to become a financially viable business.

One significant development took place toward the close of this 18-month period. The CNSB got access to a new market. Since 1975, the Government of India introduced a program for early childhood care and development called Integrated Child Development Services (ICDS). One important component of this program is to provide supplementary nutrition to children below 6 years and to pregnant and lactating mothers. The district administration of some of the districts of West Bengal agreed to buy Nutrimix to give to the children (6 months to 6 years) and pregnant and lactating mothers under the supplementary nutrition program of the ICDS program. The credentials of CINI's previous work, particularly in mitigating child malnutrition, became handy in getting access to this market. Due to this fresh marketing opportunity, the future of CNSB started looking bright. Thus, the obvious decision was to continue the operation of CNSB beyond the 18 months of the World Bank grant period as a CINI-funded activity.

Because of limited availability of funds, CNSB could not recruit any professional manager. Incidentally, one PhD student of IIMC, who became interested in this organizational transformation process of CINI toward social business, decided to work for his PhD thesis on this topic. For obtaining an insight into this process, he decided to get involved in the day-to-day running of CNSB. With his previous industry experience and assistance from another PhD student from IIMC and with their labor of love, they substantially contributed in improving the operations of CNSB.

Professionally Managed Social Business - CINCOMM

In the meantime, CINI's Board took a crucial decision, the need for which became apparent on setting up the CNSB. It was decided to create a separate nonprofit Section 25 Company, which was named "CINI Community Initiatives" (CINCOMM). It was decided that the Nutrimix social business and some other activities of CINI aiming at financial self-reliance will be under CINCOMM. Thus, the process of exploring the possibilities of "turning around" from a philanthropic to self-reliant mode obtained a formal shape through the creation of this Section 25 Company in March 2011 (now nonprofit Section 8 Company under the Companies Act, 2013).[4]

Subsequently, a management graduate from IIMC, having strong motivation toward social causes, was recruited as CEO of CINCOMM. Because of the new market in the ICDS and with improved performance, it was possible now to hire a professional manager. The new professional manager with his team of dedicated workers and with their challenging work could extend and improve the performance of CINCOMM immensely. Below, we mention some of the improvements introduced.

Firstly, the marketing opportunity of Nutrimix started expanding vastly as more and more districts in West Bengal and beyond started buying Nutrimix under the supplementary nutrition program of the ICDS. Nutrimix being developed as a low-cost nutritious calorie-dense food fitted well into that market. One great advantage was that through these government-sponsored programs, the reach of Nutrimix became widespread. The CINCOMM mainly focused on providing Nutrimix to government-sponsored food distribution under ICDS, and supplementary food distribution program undertaken by renowned NGOs and Gram Panchayats. Thus, CINCOMM mainly relied on bulk sale of Nutrimix. Nutrimix is given to pre-school children (6 months to 6 years) and pregnant and lactating mothers. Along with the need for meeting the new demand, the expansion of production of Nutrimix was felt as requiring the setting up of factories in the districts. In the beginning of the 2017, around 5,00,000 beneficiaries have been given Nutrimix daily thus having a widespread impact in mitigating malnutrition.[5]

Secondly, along with bulk production, the quality of Nutrimix has also improved immensely through adoption of improved practices in the production process. Because of bulk sales, Nutrimix is now sold in packets of 500 gm.

Finally, the most fulfilling fact is that the Nutrimix social business has started making an important contribution in mitigating child malnutrition by promoting widespread use of Nutrimix in a self-reliant manner. It was possible to support part of the expansion of Nutrimix-production capacity from the surplus generated from the Nutrimix social business. Besides, it is also helping CINI to serve social causes in a self-reliant manner by generating some surplus from its operation and reducing its donation-dependent vulnerability to an extent.

Discussion and Concluding Observations

In the above account, we have discussed how a philanthropy-based NGO has successfully moved toward self-reliance. In this concluding section, we sum up important lessons emerged from this process.

1. *The initiation of a move toward self-reliance may happen in a philanthropy-based NGO only when other sources of funding become scarce:* As donations and State grants require relatively less effort than becoming self-reliant, any philanthropy-based NGO will not try to become self-reliant so long as other types of funding are easily available.

2. *Culture of charity in a philanthropy-based NGO will resist any attempt to self-reliance:* Philanthropy and self-reliance represent two diverse types of culture. The culture of charity in a philanthropy-based NGO will resist any move toward self-reliance. This is because performing acts of charity gives a noble feeling and keeps the service provider in a position of power with less accountability, whereas becoming self-reliant demands certain skills and better performance. Hence, moving from charity to self-reliance is likely to face opposition in charity-based organization.

3. *For a philanthropy-based NGO, availability of initial capital is crucial for moving toward social business:* As moving toward self-reliance often involves initial investment for a social business, such moves are

stalled because of want of capital. Along with an aversion for moving away from the comfort zone of charity, lack of expertise in business often inhibits deploying initial capital for undertaking such venture.

4. *Whereas in a profit maximizing business, earning profit works as the driving force, in social business, the zeal to serve the social purpose in a self-reliant manner becomes the driving force:* Being based on the philosophy of philanthropy, charity-based organizations are sustained by a motivation to serve people. Being based on business methods, social business may lack a similar motivation. At the same time, a social business is devoid of the profit-earning drive of a profit maximization business. What would then be the motivating factor for a social business? The pleasant discovery of this social business experiment is that the zeal to serve a social purpose in a self-reliant manner became the driving forces and the most important contributing factor in the success of this social business. This discovery echoed Yunus's (2007, 215) observation, ". . .greed is not the only fuel for free enterprise. Social goal can replace greed as a powerful motivational force".

5. *Getting support from persons with relevant skills for the business along with compassion for a social cause is crucial for the success of social business:* The NGOs may not have persons with business skills. When NGOs move to social business, they would need persons with business and other required skills with compassion for a social cause. It is often difficult to find such people. As a way out, Dees (1998, 66) suggested "Nonprofit leaders also can reach out for pro bono consulting from volunteer business-people or from business school students". In the case of CINI, business school students made important contributions in the successful transformation to social business. Besides, it also obtained the backing of an experienced food technologist and renowned scientist in-house.

Social causes may be served more effectively through social business as has been illustrated by the product development and spread of the reach of Nutrimix in mitigating child malnutrition. However, in social business, there is a risk of deviating from serving social causes toward profit maximization, if business skill is not combined with the compassion for serving a social cause. For serving a social cause in a self-reliant manner, the need for combining a passion for serving social causes with business skills cannot be overemphasized. Lack of business skill will make self-reliance untenable, and lack of compassion for a social cause will fail such businesses to serve the social cause. In this context, the following observation of Dees (1998, 67) is very pertinent, ". . . commercial operations will not – and should not – drive out philanthropic initiatives. Many worthwhile objectives cannot effectively be pursued by relying on market mechanism alone . . . . The challenge is to harness these social impulses and marry them to the best aspects of business practice in order to create a social sector that is as effective as it can be".

Notes

1. In a judgment of the Supreme Court of India on 9th June 2017 this observation of Rajiv Gandhi was mentioned (http://indianexpress. com/article/india/rajiv-gandhis-popular-15paise-remark-finds-mention-in-sc-verdict-4696740/).
2. Member of the team lead by Dr. Subhas Mukherjee that produced world's second test tube baby.
3. Source: Nutrimix Income and Expenditure Statement, prepared by Assistant Director, Finance CINI, (December 2011).
4. "As per Section 8(1a, 1b, 1c) of the new Companies Act, 2013, a Section 8 company can be established for 'promotion of commerce, art, science, sports, education, research, social welfare, religion, charity, protection of environment or any such other object,' provided it 'intends to apply its profits, if any, or other income in promoting its objects' and 'intends to prohibit the payment of any dividend to its members.'"
5. Source: CINI NUTRIMIX – an illustrative storyline (mimeo.)

CHAPTER 3

Compassionate Business

> . . .an organization with a social mission does not have to depend on external funding; or run in a loss; or make compromises in efficiency, scale, quality, or scope.
>
> —**Mehta** and **Shenoy** *Infinite Vision*

Our discussion of the business model that we are calling as "Compassionate Business Model" is based on the example of a business model developed by the widely acclaimed Aravind Eye Care System. Aravind Eye Care System has its origin in compassion. It is out of a feeling of strong compassion toward suffering of the people, particularly the poor, due to eye-related problems, the ophthalmologist founder of Aravind Eye Care System thought of setting up an eye hospital. It is this compassionate feeling that guided the innovations in running the hospital in a self-sustaining mode, which gave birth to a profit-making compassionate business model. Thus, we will call the innovative business model developed by the Aravind Eye Care System as compassionate business model and thus, our discussion on compassionate business model in this chapter is based on Aravind Eye Care System. Our discussion of this business model is primarily based on the account written after close observation of this model by Pavithra K. Mehta and Suchitra Shenoy (2011).

3.1 Origins of Aravind Eye Care System

Dr. Govindappa Venkataswamy, the founder of Aravind Eye Care System, was an ophthalmologist by training. During his service life, he served in government hospitals in the state of Tamil Nadu, India. As government hospitals provide free treatment, patients from poor households come for treatment in considerable number to government hospitals. Thus, during his service life in government hospitals, Dr. Venkataswamy, who is popularly addressed as Dr. V, had observed closely the sufferings of the villagers from poor families, due to untreated ailments of the eyes. His growing up in a village also enabled him to witness this suffering of the villagers due to illnesses. For instance, with the process of aging, some villagers are likely to develop cataract of eyes. When a poor villager cannot afford to get the cataract treated, s/he gradually becomes blind. When a poor villager gradually becomes blind, s/he loses employment. A carpenter or a tailor or an agricultural laborer fails to get employment because of loss of eye sight due to cataract. Thus, they become a sort of burden to their poor families and lead a miserable life. As an ophthalmologist, Dr. Venkataswamy, a man of high levels of conscience, felt a strong urge of doing something to solve this problem of suffering of the poor due to this "needless blindness." Thus, when he retired from service, he set up an eleven-bedded eye hospital in his brother's residence in Madurai, in the state of Tamil Nadu, India, with the limited post retirement savings he had. This hospital has now emerged as the world's largest health service provider at affordable costs.

3.2   How Aravind Provided Free Treatment with Profit

The most significant and astonishing aspect of the Aravind model is that despite providing high-quality free service to most of its patients, it runs in profit. We would explore how Aravind made this wonderful miracle possible.

How is it possible for Aravind to provide high-quality free treatment to most of its patients, but still make profit? It is this puzzling fact that has made this model highly acclaimed. The admirers of this Aravind miracle include management expert like Peter Drucker to Nobel Laureate Muhammad Yunus, Bill Clinton to England's Princess Alexandra. It received the Gates Award for Global Health, the Hilton Humanitarian Prize, and many other recognition. The Aravind case is a mandatory reading for every MBA student at the Harvard Business School (Mehta and Shenoy 2012, 2).

In the section that follows, we will discuss how Aravind shaped the above-mentioned miracle, or how it was possible to provide high-quality free medical treatment to majority of its patients with profit. In other words, we will be discussing the shaping of what we have called compassionate business model. It may be mentioned here that this business model is particularly appropriate for developing countries with high population pressure where the majority of the poor are deprived of necessary services, including medical treatment, and where the government mostly fails to provide the required services to the poor, where poor people often are not in the position of paying for those services.

In answering to the quarries of a British Journalist on how Aravind achieved the miracle of making profit despite providing free treatment to the majority of its patients, Dr. Govindappa Venkataswamy, the founder of Aravind, once said: ". . .we did good-quality work, so the rich people came and paid us, and we could treat the poor people with the money saved. The poor people brought more poor people; the rich people brought more rich people. So now, here we are" (Mehta and Shenoy 2012, 7–8). This explanation in a way gives the gist of the operation of the Aravind model.

Of course, the going was not that simple. In achieving this miracle, a lot of innovative steps were taken. Some of the principles and innovative steps that contributed to the success of Aravind are discussed below. Above all, a keen sense of compassion remained the driving force of all enabling principles and innovations.

Striving for High-volume Service

Proactively Reaching the Poor Patients

When Aravind started its journey, it found that despite referring many patients for free surgery to their hospital, after screening them on visiting villages, many did not report to get treatment, though it was offered free of cost by Aravind. The Aravind management was puzzled. They started enquiring why many patients were not coming to get their eye ailments treated despite offering free treatment. What they discovered was as follows. Poor patients told them that for getting cataract treated, they need to travel to Madurai from their village. Usually, another person needs to escort the patient, as after the operation, the patient's eyes will be bandaged and s/he will not be able to see. Thus, the patient would need to meet the travel expenses and boarding and lodging expenses in Madurai for two people. On top of it, as they will be absent from work during that period, they will not get wages for those days. The patient needs to have the funds for meeting all those expenses. As the patients from the poor families often did not have that type of savings, they were unable to avail free treatment offered by Aravind. Thus, it was realized by Aravind that just providing free treatment was not enough; the poor patients need to be enabled to avail the free treatment. This also shows just having an intention to serve the poor is inadequate, one needs to learn about the reality of the world of the poor and should have the depth of compassion to take up the challenge in enabling the poor to overcome the difficult reality in which they live.

Aravind's endeavor always has been to provide treatment to as many patients as possible. Origin of this principle is the compassion of treating anyone seeking treatment, irrespective of the paying capacity of the patient. Dr. Venkataswamy once observed (Mehta and Shenoy 2012, 14), "Our focus is on human welfare, if a man can't pay me, it does not matter. He will give later if he can". This reflects humane attitude – faith in the goodness of human beings, of the founder of Aravind. It is intriguing to see how based on this type of value system, Aravind flourished as a good surplus making organization.

The principle of providing service in high volume should not be viewed as just a policy adopted by Aravind; it has its origin in a value or commitment to "eradicate all needless blindness" from which particularly poor people in rural India and in other developing countries suffer, mainly because of untreated cataract and other ailments of the eye. It is rooted in a value propagated by Dr. V. He wrote, "To some of us bringing divine consciousness to our daily activities is our Goal. The Hospital work gives an opportunity for this spiritual growth. In your growth, you widen your consciousness and you feel the suffering of others in you." (Mehta and Shenoy 2012, 27).

Aravind's motto has been to get rid of needless blindness. Thus, it proactively tries to reach as many patients as possible. One important mechanism for doing that is to organize camps for eye check-up. These camps are generally organized at locations where eye treatment is not easily available. These camps are organized in collaboration with the local community. The community provides space for conducting eye camps and gets the patients; doctors from Aravind provide the required treatment at the eye camps, free of cost. The majority of these patients require surgery. Patients requiring surgery are referred to Aravind hospitals. Taking the patients to the hospital, performing the operation, providing boarding and lodging during their treatment period, and bringing them back to their village – this entire process is arranged by the Aravind, free of cost. Thus, a proactive compassion for reaching as many patients possible through this mechanism contributed in providing treatment in high volume. That Aravind has emerged as treating the highest number of patients in the world at low cost is imbedded in its value system.

Converting High-volume Service into High-quality Service

Interestingly, a remarkable innovation made by Aravind is, converting high-volume service as an enabler to provide high-quality service and also making profit. The miracle of translating the increase in the volume of patients into efficiency and high-quality service has been possible through some unique innovations. We discuss below two such innovations.

Creating Intensively Trained Cadre of Paraprofessionals

For providing high-volume and the best treatment to its patients, Aravind made an innovation of creating a cadre of paraprofessionals. After studying the entire process of eye surgery from the entry to the discharge of a patient, the tasks involved were broken down. Some of the tasks typically done by the ophthalmologist, but may not need that level of expertise were identified. Those tasks were assigned to intensively trained paraprofessionals. This enables the patients to get individualized attention at a reduced cost and, at the same time, contributed to the productive time of the doctors. Thus, Aravind enabled the ophthalmologists to be more productive by freeing them from some of the time-consuming routine chores and thus "allow these doctors to focus almost exclusively on diagnosing patients and performing operations."

Aravind has designed a 2-year residential training program for the paraprofessionals, on successful completion of which, they are offered permanent employment for 3 years. Usually, village girls, who have completed their high school and in the age group of 17 to 19, are recruited for this training program. A metamorphosis takes place among these girls after they involve themselves in this training program. As most of the patients at Aravind come from rural Tamil Nadu, the patients feel at home with these paraprofessionals who speak their language.

There is a high turnover of the nurses at Aravind. When they come to Aravind, they are fresh out of high school. As per the local custom, their families arrange for their marriage another 4 or 5 years later after graduating from high school. As a result, they get relocated where their husbands live; hence, they are not able to continue with their job at Aravind. This helps the Aravind to keep the average age of this workforce young and Aravind continues to obtain the services of a young energetic workforce.

This also brings a transformation in the lives of these girls and their siblings. If they were not hired by Arvind, they would have been engaged in grazing cattle or taken up a low-paying job in a factory or would have been forced to getting married early. Working at Aravind for 5 years also help these girls, mostly from rural backgrounds, to have an earning, which becomes financially handy for their families, including for meeting the wedding-related expenses of these girls. This army of paraprofessionals is the pivot of Aravind Hospitals. Thus, this innovation, apart from contributing to Arvind's service efficiency, contributes in bringing a beneficial transformation in the life of these rural girls.

Assembly-line Techniques in Operation Theater

At Aravind Eye Hospitals (AEH), there has been a continuous attempt in streamlining the entire process from registration of the patient to screening, to operating where needed, to discharging the patients. This attempt has resulted in reducing the waiting time of the patients. For instance, when a patient is advised to have surgery, the patient is admitted on the same day and operated the very next day.

Typically, an ophthalmologist would do the basic vision testing, a preliminary examination, measurement of ocular pressure, pupil dilation, and a final examination before surgery. For more fruitful utilization of the time of the ophthalmologist and for helping them to be more productive, at Aravind, most of these tasks are performed by an intensively trained cadre of paraprofessionals. For enhancing the surgeon's productivity, Aravind practiced assembly-line techniques in the operation theater.

Below we quote a description of workflow in the surgical ward (Prahlad 2005, 276) to get an idea of how assembly-line techniques shape the workflow in the operation theater for higher productivity of the doctors.

At 7 A.M., the doctors are in their surgical gowns and masks. The names of the patients to be operated on during the day in each theater are put up . . . The nursing staff arrives at 6.30 A.M., and the patients for the day are moved to a ward adjacent to operating theaters. The patients to be operated on soon are given local anesthetic injections and their eyes are washed and disinfected. By 7:15 A.M., two patients are on two adjacent operating tables. In general, in many hospitals, two operating tables are not kept in an operation theater because of presumed risk of infections. However, AEH has been following the system of having more than one table in an operation theater from its inception and has not had any problems . . .

The operation theater has four operating tables, laid out side-by-side. Two doctors operate, each on two adjacent tables. By the time the first operation is over, the second patient is ready with the microscope focused on the eye to be operated on. The first patient is bandaged by the nurses and moved out. The third patient, who has in the meanwhile been moved in. . ., is sitting on a bench in the theater. As soon as the first patient moves out, the third patient is put on the first table and prepared for the operation. As soon as the second patient is finished, the doctor moves back to the first table, with virtually no loss of time. He is constantly moving between the two tables, with hardly any break. In the same way, another doctor operates on the third and fourth tables . . .

Usually, no surgeries are done in the afternoon. The theaters are scrubbed and cleaned and the instruments are sterilized.

Mehta and Shenoy (2012,18) have rightly observed:

> The hospital-as-factory mindset can raise logical objections in the uninitiated, but the reality is that Aravind's approach serves patients' interest in multiple ways. The streamlined workflow increases efficiency, which means less waiting time. Task repetition creates competence, which means better clinical outcomes. And employing skilled paraprofessionals for steps that do not require doctor's expertise not only facilitates individualized attention, but also reduces prices. All three factors working in conjunction contribute to scale and affordability while improving patient experience and the quality-of-care.

Additionally, the above process adds to the expertise and experience of the doctors, strengthening a noble feeling of service in them. In general, a patient can approach a doctor only when s/he is able to pay the fees for the treatment. Thus, doctors normally do not get the opportunity to treat that section of patients who are not able to pay. In developing countries, this group constitutes a large section of the patients. Thus, in a developing country so long as a doctor treats only those who can pay, doctors get a limited exposure to the variety of patients they get to treat. As in Aravind Hospitals, doctors get the opportunity to treat paying and nonpaying patients in their high-volume treatments, they get to see not only more number of patients, but also patients of greater diversity. This contributes to the expertise and high-quality treatment offered at Aravind. This enabling system of providing high-quality treatment to the poor patients for free, along with services to the paying patients, gives a noble feeling of having done service to the poor among the doctors and other staff members of Aravind and contributes to their job satisfaction.

The above innovation is remarkable in several ways. Below, we mention some of the contributions of the above innovation.

Firstly, as the doctors perform repetitive tasks several times, they become more efficient and more productive. In this context, the following observation of Mehta and Shenoy (2012, 44) is pertinent, "In many settings, quality and quantity are assumed to have an inverse relationship. Several research studies in the medical field, and specifically in cataract surgery, validate what most surgeons know to be true: the more you do, the better you get".

Secondly, as the paramedical staff takes care of pre-operative and post-operative care, patients receive better-quality and personalized service by the nursing staff.

Thirdly, the above innovations facilitate better and optimum utilization of the services of the surgeons along with the intensive involvement of the paramedical staff. Better-quality operations are thus, performed in higher numbers at reduced costs.

Fourthly, the innovations mentioned above played a key role in enabling Aravind to make profit despite providing free treatment to majority of its patients. Let me present a simplistic explanation of how that became possible. The said innovations enabled the surgeons at Aravind to be more productive without wasting of time in between surgeries. Also, the intensive use of their productive time was made possible being assisted by the efficient nursing staff. As a result, productivity of the surgeons at Aravind is more than five times the national average. For instance, while an eye surgeon in India performs 400 surgeries in average in a year, Aravind surgeons perform more than 2,000 surgeries in average in a year. Those 400 surgeries performed by eye surgeons in hospitals in India are paid surgeries and with that type of productivity of surgeons, those eye hospitals run in profit. From this, we can assume that if out of all the surgeries performed by the surgeons in Aravind in a year, 400 surgeries are paid for, then Aravind also should be able to run in profit. In Aravind, 40 percent of the patients pay for their treatment. This number is 800 (40 percent of 2,000), which is double than the number of paid patients required for making a profit. Hence, it is not at all surprising that Aravind makes a profit, despite providing free treatment to the majority (60 percent) of its patients.

Thus, we observe that the above innovations not only enabled Aravind to provide treatment to a large number of patients, but also the very process of providing service to more patients enabled it to provide better-quality treatment and the same process enabled Aravind to make profit.

This is a very significant innovation in the promotion of social development in populous developing countries where so many people suffer due to unavailability of basic amenities and where providing services to a multitude of people is viewed as a barrier to providing superior-quality service. In this context, the following observation about Aravind is very significant,

> When patient numbers go up, even if it's on the nonpaying side, Aravind becomes more effective. While this seems counter intuitive from a financial perspective, everything at Aravind, from the marketing of its services and hands-on training of its medical personnel, to the steady workflow in its operating room and its data-driven quality improvement systems, benefits from, and in many ways hinges on, Aravind's high influx of nonpaying patients.

Thulsi Ravilla, Aravind's first managerial hire says, "It doesn't happen by accident, we design for it" (Mehta and Shenoy 2012, 30–31).

In most of the developing countries, poor people depend on government hospitals for treatment, as free treatment is available only at government hospitals. As government hospitals provide free treatment and as the number of government hospitals is less in comparison with the number of patients to be treated, these hospitals are always overcrowded. The overcrowding of the government hospitals is most commonly cited as a cause for deficiency of services provided by them, because of which poor people are the worst sufferers. Here, in Aravind, we find a unique case where the increasing number of nonpaying patients has been transformed into an advantage and has helped improve the quality of service! Thus, Metha and Shenoy (2012, 44) made a significant observation regarding the overcrowded government hospitals of developing countries, where overcrowding is commonly cited as a cause of inefficient service, that "Aravind's own work consistently demonstrates that high-quality medical care can be fostered, and not undermined, by an enormous patient load."

Differential Pricing

Aravind Eye Hospitals follow a differential pricing policy. Patients are offered a choice of opting for accommodation ranging from an air-conditioned private room to a nonprivate room to free-shared accommodations and also choosing elective surgery. A patient gets a choice to opt for free treatment or for a paid treatment of a selected category. Aravind Eye Hospitals believe that (Mehta and Shenoy 2012, 76) "a pricing model offering free service as one option within a broader range can serve more patients in need than a system that does only charity." For opting for free treatment, no documentation is required thus, respecting the patients' honor. Paying patients can exercise a choice of the type of surgery and quality of accommodations they want. Quality of treatment provided to paying and nonpaying patients is the same. The ratio of nonpaying to those paying market rates at Aravind is around 60:40. While paying and nonpaying ratio is not fixed, it is closely monitored.

> If either end loses faith in Aravind's services, the entire ecosystem of the organization is thrown off balance. Losing free patients increases unit costs, affects Aravind's reputation in the community, and reduces training capacity. Losing paying patients augurs a different set of ills. The organization knows this from walking the delicate balance between the two (Mehta and Shenoy 2012, 81).

This mechanism of differential pricing has helped Aravind to maintain not only financial self-sustenance, it also takes care of capital expenditure for all expansions and new units (Prahalad 2005, 269).

Cost Reduction

Cost cutting and frugal entrepreneurship have been one important part of Aravind's operations. In a way, this is also a consequence of a sense of compassion. As Aravind endeavored to provide treatment to whoever comes for services, irrespective of his or her paying capability, Aravind does not have a chance to become an extravagant organization. It actively practiced frugal entrepreneurship. There are many examples of this austerity at Aravind. Let me mention some.

The utilization of the existing equipment and infrastructure at Aravind is very high. For instance, this ratio between actual use and maximum potential use of existing infrastructure is globally 25 percent within eye care service. At Aravind, this ratio is around 80 percent (Mehta and Shenoy 2012, 88).

Further, due to problems regarding repair service and availability of spare parts, 50 percent of medical equipment in developing countries is unusable or under repair. For overcoming this problem, Aravind has created an efficient in-house maintenance division.

Let me cite examples of austerity practiced at Aravind Hospital, Madurai. Aravind provides accommodation to patients who undergo operation at Aravind hospital at Madurai. Managing this facility also follows many cost-cutting and frugal measures. We will cite just one example from the housekeeping section. The beds in this accommodation are expectedly provided with bed sheets. When those bed sheets become old and little worn out, they are not discarded instantly. Those little worn out bed sheets are then made into table cloths or window curtains of those rooms. When those table cloths or curtains become further old, they are used as mopping clothes. This is just one example of frugality and sustainability practices, which is in the DNA of Aravind that has contributed to its success.

In the above-mentioned guest house, there is a canteen in the ground floor, primarily to cater to the patients and their accompanied persons who are provided accommodation in that building as needed. The patients and their accompanied persons can have food in this canteen. This is a neat, clean and well-managed canteen, charging reasonable rates. There is a big dining hall in this canteen. When the customers come to this canteen, they are requested to occupy tables near the place where other customers have occupied seats. This type of monitoring of seat occupancy by the customers is done for optimizing the use of ceiling fans by putting on fans only in the areas occupied by customers and thus, preventing any wastage in the use of electric energy. In appropriate places in the dining hall, a message requesting the customers to switch off the fans and lights, when not required, is written. To make the message more appealing and educating, facts on per electrical appliance wise power consumption usage is mentioned. This not only saves energy, but also educates the customers on the need of energy conservation. Additionally, this monitoring of seating facilitates providing service to the customers by the serving staff, reducing their need of movement for serving, and saves serving time. If the customers occupied seats in a scattered manner, none of these could have been possible. The canteen is run by a private party, but association with the Aravind has brought these better practices in its operation.

Introducing Intraocular Lens and Setting Up Aurolab

Making treatment affordable to people, particularly, to the poor by cost reduction should be viewed as an integral part of Arvind's values of compassion and self-sustenance. It is not just a matter of cost cutting. Cost cutting may be the just the outer manifestation, but it is imbibed in the values of compassion, a strong urge to make the best treatment available to all and the urge to become a self-sustaining organization. Aravind's endeavor in manufacturing intraocular lens and ultimately setting up the production unit, the Aurolab, reflects all these values of Aravind.

In 1976, when Aravind was founded in India, cataract patients were given aphakic surgery. Aphakic surgery involved removing the clouded cataract lens. To replace the lost focusing mechanism, patients were given heavy spectacles with a high refractive power. By the 1980s, invention of intraocular lens (IOL) brought dramatic transformation across the Western world in cataract surgery. In this surgery, of removing clouded cataract lens, IOLs were implanted in the eye. The implanted lenses could be tailored to the precise power required for each individual eye, thus discarding the need for wearing glasses. However, it took time for arrival of IOL technology in India, and Aravind played a crucial role in bringing this advanced technology to India. Due to their value orientation doctors at Aravind felt that IOL is more relevant to poor people belonging to working class for whom to work with a heavy glass after cataract surgery becomes very inconvenient. However, the prohibitive cost of IOL prevented Aravind to provide IOL free of cost. However, rich people who could afford it, opted for IOL surgery at Aravind by paying for it. Thus, the situation was such that the poor patients, belonging to working class who would have benefited most by IOL, had to opt for free aphakic surgery for cataract whereas rich people opted for IOL surgery as paying patients. This was against Aravind's value system of providing the best treatment to all, irrespective of being rich or poor. However, prohibitive cost of IOL which had to be imported from abroad prevented them to do the same. The only way out was to reduce the cost of the IOL by manufacturing it in India. For Arvind, the challenge was also to reduce its manufacturing cost, so that it could be offered free of cost to the poor patients.

Aravind took up the challenge by setting up its own manufacturing unit "Aurolab" and started manufacturing of IOL in the face of opposition from many quarters. Not only was it successful in manufacturing IOL, it could also reduce the manufacturing cost of IOL substantially and could offer subsidized IOL surgery at around $10 when just the price of imported IOL was around $80 to $100 (Mehta and Shenoy 2012,156). Aurolab not only started manufacturing IOL, soon it also started producing some other medicines and equipments required for the eye hospital. Aravind's policy of self-sourcing also helped the hospital to reduce its operational cost. Setting up of Aurolab and its independent successful operation are in line with Aravind's principles of differential pricing and providing cross-subsidy to serve the needy. This is another hallmark of Aravind. Aurolab produced "a revolution - that one is rooted in, and driven by, compassion."

To conclude, the Aravind Eye Care System is based on compassion. This compassion has driven this system to undertake the mission of "to eradicate all needless blindness". As it is the poor people who suffer most from this needless blindness, Aravind proactively attempted to provide free and the best treatment to them. This involved providing high-volume, high-quality free treatment to the poor. Through certain innovations, Aravind converted high-volume treatment into high-quality treatment. With differential pricing, it could cross-subsidize the free or highly subsidize treatment for the poor with financial viability. Along with cost cutting, frugal entrepreneurship was another hall mark of Aravind. Setting up Aurolab was part of that which enabled Aravind to make the best treatment affordable to the poor. Thus, the Aravind model presents a unique example of a business model most suitable for promoting social development in less-developed countries in a sustainable way.

CHAPTER 4

Business Based on Microcredit

While discussing the concept of "social business," Yunus (2007, 28) mentioned that there are two kinds of social businesses. In an earlier chapter on social business, we have mainly discussed about one type of social business, that which aims at solving social problems through its business operations and thereby serves the interest of the poor. Apart from this type of social business, Yunus has mentioned about another type of social business – a profit-maximizing business that is owned by the poor. This type of business may or may not create social benefits, but the families of the poor benefit from any profit made by such a business. Thus, according to Yunus, business owned by the poor, through the mechanism of microcredit is a type of social business. In fact, Yunus arrived at the concept of social business through his work on microcredit.

Yunus (2007, 113–115) observed that poor people have several needs to be met like those relating to education, health care, sanitation, infrastructure, housing etc. to improve their living condition. However, it is the need for credit that should be met first. He observes that human beings have an innate skill for survival and that is why poor are still alive. Credit enables them to make use of their skills for better living.

4.1 Origins of Microcredit

We will briefly describe how Muhammad Yunus realized the importance of credit in removing extreme poverty. In June 1972, Yunus returned to his native country, Bangladesh from the United States where he had gone to pursue higher studies. He joined the Economics Department at Chittagong University in Bangladesh to teach Economics. This university was in a rural area. Bangladesh was passing through an economically tough time then. Moved by the poverty of the people in the neighborhood, Yunus thought of doing something to remove poverty.

He first thought of alleviating hunger by increasing agricultural productivity by taking initiative of providing irrigation facilities to the farmers. That initiative increased agricultural productivity, but failed to benefit the very poor, who were landless. The landless constituted the majority of the poor. Thus, Yunus realized that agricultural development, which is a land-based activity, may leave out most of the poor population, who do not possess any land.

Yunus observed that these groups of rural poor, a vast majority of whom are landless, make a living and try to survive through hard labor primarily through self-employment. But unfortunately, they remain in abject poverty because they lack the needed capital for undertaking income-generating activities. They need to borrow capital from the local money lender with very high interest for undertaking income-generating activities. Thus, whatever income they get through their hard labor goes in paying back the interest of the capital. Thus, they continue to remain in poverty despite working very hard. For instance, poor women work all day long for making bamboo stools, but she needs to buy the bamboo for her stools from the local money lender under the condition to sell the stools at a price offered by him, which is very low. She may need a small amount for which she does not have any other access. Commercial banks follow a norm of providing loans only against collateral. Thus, commercial banks offer loans to only those who can provide collateral, the rich. As poor women are not able to provide collateral, they cannot obtain a loan from the commercial banks. Thus, the poor women need to borrow from the money lender with high interest, in the terms dictated by him. In this exploitative process, she gets very little income despite her hard labor. This is a type of slave labor, which keeps them in abject poverty.

Along with reduced employment opportunity due to increasing mechanization of agriculture, rural and urban poor are also deprived of educational opportunity and occupational skills. Thus, usually they have very limited opportunities to get wage employment. As it is not possible to provide wage employment for everyone, self-employment has a scope. It has some advantages over wage employment. It frees a person from welfare dependency. Average cost of creating self-employment job is lower than creating wage employment. It is also more flexible.

Thus, Yunus proposes the creation of microcredit programs to enable the poor to overcome poverty by becoming self-employed. From his observation in the field, Yunus also realized that apart from jobs, self-employment is an important option for the poor to tide over poverty. Yunus observes that though skill training is important, "the best strategy is to let people's natural abilities blossom before we introduce new skills to them." Yunus (2008, 54) believed that entrepreneurial ability is present in every individual. He thus, argued that by providing opportunity for becoming an entrepreneur to everyone, it is possible to eradicate poverty. Microcredit can play a crucial role here by providing opportunity to the poor to become self-employed. Thus alleviating poverty through business is the core element of the microcredit program.

4.2   How Microcredit Operates

Various models of microcredit programs are in operation. Let us briefly describe how the microcredit mechanism typically operates through "self-help groups" (SHG). Often a self-help group (SHG) is formed by the women from low-income communities consisting of 10 to 12 women. These groups are often formed with support from NGOs, commercial banks, or microfinance institutions. The group members save a small amount on a regular basis, which is collected by a designated group member. This type of savings of a small amount on a regular basis continues for a specified period. Purpose of this is to create a regular savings habit among the members of the group. Through this process, a fund is created by the self-help group members. Members of the group then can borrow an amount by turn as required and as decided by the group for undertaking income-generating activities. The borrower members are supposed to return the borrowed amount with interest in regular installments as decided by the group. Here, often the liability of returning the borrowed amount by the borrowing members rests on all the members of the group. Thus, an attempt is made to create an informal group pressure on the borrowing members for timely return of the borrowed amount. Returning borrowed amount in time provides an access to future loans of bigger amounts. This also works as an incentive to return loan in time. All members get an opportunity to take a loan from this fund by turn. The group usually opens an account in the bank for this purpose, where this fund is kept. In this way, being enabled to take a loan at a relatively lower interest without any collateral and undertaking income-generating activities, the poor people can increase their income, repay their loan, and come out of poverty.

Thus, poor people form a group to create a fund of their own, from which they take credit to undertake income-generating activities. Formation of a group was found very crucial in loan delivery-recovery. Individually, a poor person feels very insecure in saving, taking loan, and repaying. Becoming a member of a group creates group support. Peer pressure also helps in maintaining discipline in saving and loan recovery. For the poor, the policy of saving and repaying in tiny amounts on a regular basis is also helpful.

It has been found from experience that when income of a women member of the household increases, that benefits the entire family, which is not necessarily true with the increase of income of the men members of the poor households. Thus, self-help groups are generally formed with the women members of the poor households aiming at generating income among them.

Thus, microfinance and, specifically, microcredit enables the poor household to undertake income-generating activities to come out of poverty. Thus, microcredit is a good example of how business can be a useful tool for poverty alleviation.

The term 'microcredit' which was a popular terminology of the mid-1990s has been replaced by 'microfinance'. Microfinance refers to a wide range of financial services aimed at the poor. These includes not only credit but also savings and other financial services such as insurance and money transfer.

There are different mechanisms through which the delivery of micro-credits operates. The different microcredit models are given below.

A) Self-help Group Model or SHG Model

The Self-Help Groups are promoted by Self Help Promotional Institutions (SHPIs). A SHPI can be NGOs, financial institutions, government agency or an individual. SHPIs promote Self-help Groups to organize the poor for encouraging thrift. The SHPI promote and nurture SHGs till they become independent and self-sustainable entities.

B) SHG Federation Model

When the number of SHGs increases it becomes difficult for SHPI to interface with each group directly. At this stage, SHPI starts thinking of setting up an apex body that can act as intermediary between SHPI and the SHGs. These apex institutions aggregate savings from SHGs and borrow funds on its strength from external agencies, banks or other financial institutions. Federations act as intermediaries between financial institutions and SHGs.

C) The Grameen Bank Model

To alleviate poverty through microcredit, Yunus created a bank for the poor in 1983. This bank was named as Grameen Bank. This bank provides credit to poor women without collateral. For taking loan from Grameen Bank, women are required to form a group of five friends. All the members of the group should approve the loan application. Though the respective borrower is responsible to repay the loan, the group functions as a social network in providing assistance in business and loan repayment. Ten to twelve such groups meet weekly at a center where loan repayments are collected, application for new loans are submitted.

D) Joint Liability Group Model

A joint Liability Group (JLG) is an informal group comprising preferably 4 to 10 individuals coming together for the purpose of availing bank loan either singly or through the group mechanism against their mutual guarantee. The JLG members would offer a joint undertaking to the bank that enables them to avail loans. The JLG members are expected to engage in similar type of economic activities. Intended borrowers involved in similar occupations and residing in close proximity from Joint Liability Group.

E) Individual Model

This is a normal traditional credit delivery system where MFI is directly linked with the individual for extending financial services and charged for the same.

4.3   Spread of Microcredit

Yunus (2008, 66) points out:

> The microcredit idea, which began in the village of Jobra in
> Bangladesh, has spread around the globe. There are now micro-
> credit programs in almost every country in the world. Microcredit
> has made the greatest inroads in Asia. But, it also has a foothold in
> countries of Africa, Latin America, and the Middle East. Micro-
> credit has also begun to operate among the poor in many coun-
> tries of the developed world, including the United States.

That poor people can come out of poverty by undertaking business
has been well established by the microcredit revolution. The significant
role of microcredit was evident when the first Microcredit Summit was
held in Washington, DC in 1997. This Summit was attended by nearly
3,000 delegates from 137 countries representing microcredit programs of
many kinds and sizes (Yunus 2008, 87). Since then, the role of business
in removing poverty through the spread of microcredit has been evident.
The 18th Microcredit Summit was held in Abu Dhabi, March 15 to 17,
2016. The Microcredit Summit Campaign (2016) explained the role of
microfinance as follows:

> Microfinance is the extension of small loans to the very poor, in com-
> bination with other financial services such as savings facilities, train-
> ing, health services, networking, and peer support. This allows them
> to pursue entrepreneurial projects that generate extra income thus,
> helping them to better provide for themselves and their families.

> In this way, microfinance allows families to work to end their own
> poverty – with dignity. Microfinance programs around the world,
> using a variety of models, have shown that poor people achieve
> strong repayment records – often higher than those of conven-
> tional borrowers. Repayment rates are high because, through a
> system of peer support used in many microcredit models, borrow-
> ers are responsible for each other's success and ensure that every
> member of the group is able to pay back their loans.

4.4   Impact of Microcredit

Does microcredit enable the poor to improve their income? Let us look at some observations. Bandhan, a successful microfinance institution in India, which has emerged as a bank, asked the Indian Institute of Management Ahmedabad for an impact study on its microfinance activities and related development programs on the lives of the underprivileged. It was found that the average annual net income of a household from all sources increased by Rs 13,231 ($207) representing a 13.81 percent rise. The borrowers' families increased their ownership of nonfarm business assets by Rs 15,558 ($243) on average, and could also generate, on average, 35.82 man days per annum of fulltime employment for family members. Another study by Abhijit Banerjee and Esther Duflo of Massachusetts Institute of Technology on Bandhan found a 15 percent increase in household consumption, and positive impacts on other measures of household wealth and welfare, such as emotional well-being (quoted in Bandyopadhyay 2016, 81– 82). However, the same authors (along with some other coauthors) (Banerjee et al. 2015, 52), in a study, were critical about the role of microcredit. Based on their analysis, they concluded:

> Thus, microcredit plays its role as a financial product in an environment where access to both credit and saving opportunities is limited. It expands households' abilities to make different intertemporal choices, including business investment. The only mistake that the microcredit enthusiasts may have made is to overestimate the potential of businesses for the poor, both as a source of revenue and as a means of empowerment for their female owners.

However, the spread of microcredit the world over demonstrates the role of business, even of a tiny business, in alleviating poverty in a self-sustaining manner. The important aspect of microcredit-based business is that it enables the very poor to come out of poverty. The point to be noted that the microcredit-based business has emerged as a mechanism of earning in the hands of women who are very poor. Even if microcredit-based business has limited capacity in generating income, its significance cannot be ignored in empowering women economically to an extent. However it is through our experience of microcredit revolution, that we now realized that economic empowerment does not automatically empower women in a society. Empowerment of women is strongly rooted in culture, and economic empowerment by itself is not enough to bring a change in the status of women solely. If the economic empowerment failed to empower women socially the way it was expected, this only points out to our limited understanding of socio-economic processes, and not of microcredit. Microcredit demonstrated the widespread role of business in poverty alleviation.

CHAPTER 5

Cooperative Business

That the profit maximization business that resulted from the capitalist philosophy is problematic for society has been realized time and again. In a search for a remedy, various other forms of businesses have been invented from time to time. Cooperative business is one such form invented by Robert Owen (1771 to 1858). Appalled by the exploitation of workers in the early stage of the industrial revolution, Owen suggested the cooperative business form, wherein workers and consumers jointly owned and managed the business, thus, benefiting all. He conceived a cooperative as a self-supporting community where producers and consumers were one and the same people. He urged production by voluntary associations for the use of consumers and not for profit. One characteristic of cooperative form of business activity is the absence of any special capital-providing class (Florence 1972, 391). Owen opened stores at his own mills in Scotland where high-quality goods were sold at prices just above cost, made possible through bulk purchases, and the savings were passed on to the workers. This was the starting point of the cooperative movement. The cooperative movement has been organized under the principle of owning and operating a business by the customers for primarily benefiting the customers rather than generating profit for the merchants. Cooperative has been defined by the International Cooperative Alliance (1995) as "an autonomous association of persons united voluntarily to meet their common economic, social and cultural needs and aspirations through a jointly owned and democratically controlled enterprise".

What role do cooperatives play in alleviating poverty? Forming a cooperative society by the marginalized sections for undertaking income-generating activities is one important way of enhancing income by overcoming exploitation. There are cooperative societies of diverse types. Here, we are particularly referring to cooperative societies formed by the poor for undertaking income-generating activities for enhancing their income. The main mechanism here is to get operational advantages in undertaking income-generating activities through collective actions of many individual operators, who are poor, and thus, enhancing their income.

Birchall (2003, 7) has summed up the role of cooperatives in developed and developing countries as follows:

> . . .cooperatives begin by enabling people to rise themselves above poverty, but later they became a means by which low- and middle-income people continued to accumulate economic advantages. They raised whole classes of people out of poverty and prevented them from slipping back into it, which in its own terms is an achievement. Sometimes this meant that poorer people were unable to benefit. At other times, the open membership principle meant that poor did benefit, but not as a part of a planned design. Cooperatives were not designed as tools of poverty reduction, but were means by which groups of people could gain economic advantages that individually they could not achieve.

7.1   Evidence of Role of Cooperatives in Poverty Alleviation

Dos cooperatives alleviate poverty? To find an answer we would look at some case studies of cooperative societies in different countries. Below, we briefly discuss those case studies from Bangladesh (Birchall 2003, 35-37), Bolivia (Birchall 2003, 44-48) and India (Kurien 2005).

Dairy Cooperatives in Bangladesh

In Bangladesh, the majority of the farmers are poor and they live in abject poverty. One way of increasing their income is creating an additional income-generating activity. Dairy farming is one such suitable activity.

Thus, after independence in 1974, the government of Bangladesh set up the Bangladesh Cooperative Milk Producers Union as a part of Cooperative Dairy Development Program with financial and technical support from international donor agencies. This program was known by its brand name "Milk Vita." The aim of setting up this cooperative union was to create supplementary income to farmers and supply better-quality milk in hygienic conditions to urban areas. Cooperatives were organized at two ends – at the level of milk-producing farmers and for selling milk to the urban dwellers. These cooperatives were run by the civil servants. It was found that they were running at a loss. Then in the year 1990, the government withdrew and the cooperative were run by a new board elected by the primary village cooperative societies. It became the farmers-owned cooperative. Management of the cooperatives shifted from civil servants to farmers organizations. They appointed managers to run the cooperatives who were accountable to the farmers' organizations. With this change in the management structure, Milk Vita started making profit. The income of the farmers increased ten-fold and enabled the consumers also to get better-quality milk.

A Water Cooperative in Bolivia

One of the Millennium Development Goals is to halve the number of people having no access to safe drinking water. There is an urgent need to invest for providing safe drinking water. Since the mid-1980s, there has been a trend to involve private, for profit organizations for providing safe drinking water. However, in Santacruz, Bolivia, a cooperative alternative to solve the problem of providing safe drinking water has been developed. This is known as SAGUAPAC and has been operating since 1979. A study undertaken by the Birmingham University found that it is one of the most efficiently run water companies in Latin America. It has low level of water leakage, elevated level of workers productivity, high level of tariff collection, and universal metering. The cooperative structure is the main reason for its efficiency. This cooperative shield its mangers from political interference to which municipal water companies are vulnerable. It allows continuity in administration, and the electoral system works as a check in corruption.

Milk Cooperative in India

There are success stories of cooperative societies in alleviating poverty in many countries of the world. The Kaira District Cooperative Milk Producers Union Limited (KDCMPUL) in India which is popularly known as Amul is one such success story. We will briefly narrate below the Amul story to illustrate the role of cooperatives in poverty alleviation.

Amul is a cooperative of milk-producing farmers. The success of this cooperative is largely due to its democratic structure. In each village of the Kaira district of Gujarat, India, milk-producing farmers have formed their own milk cooperative society together. Members of these cooperative societies elect a managing committee, which guides the society. The chairmen of these managing committees form the general body of the district cooperative union. This general body elects their board of directors, which runs the district union and the dairy plant.

The other crucial factor in the success of Amul is that it had the backing of a Gandhian and an influential political leader belonging to the Congress Party, Shri Tribhuvandas Patel, who was the leader of the dairy farmers. Tribhuvandas successfully persuaded a very efficient technocrat, Dr. Verghese Kurian to join KDCMPUL as its General Manager. Thus, began the success story of Amul.

To get an idea about some of the operating principles of Amul, we quote Kurian below. Kurien (2005, 56) observed:

> As the Chief Executive of their cooperative, my main goal became to ensure the best deal for the farmers, . . . without exploiting the consumer. The best way to do this was, of course, to give the consumer products of extremely high quality and that is what we at Amul worked hard to do. . . . There could have been no production of anything unless it was marketed at a price advantageous to those who produced it, which provided them with an incentive to produce more and more . . . the business was to maximise the price paid for the milk, not in order to maximise the dividend, as in the case of private sector. We did this by manufacturing value-added products which allowed us to give farmers a higher milk price every year.

It is important to take note of a few points in the above-mentioned strategy followed by Amul. Amul aimed at giving a better deal to the farmers based on some principles. It was not done with the aim of maximizing dividend, neither was it done by exploiting the customers. Giving a better deal to the farmers was done by manufacturing value-added products of high quality. This also encouraged the farmers to produce more. Thus, we observe that there is some similarity between cooperative business and social business. The goal of cooperative business is to maximize the gain of its producers without exploiting the consumers. Goal of social business is to serve a social cause. None of these businesses emphasize on just profit maximization.

The case studies of a cooperative show that when cooperatives are participatory, they are successful, and, for poverty reduction, cooperatives are a better alternative than for-profit organizations. Cooperatives essentially function as member-driven business organizations and need to be utilized for poverty alleviation and social development.

CHAPTER 6

Bottom of the Pyramid Business

The sight of a poor woman in a remote village in Asia or in some other remote corners of the world talking in a cell phone, or a small village shop in a poor locality in a remote corner of the world selling shampoo or biscuits or some other eatable items in a small sachet are very common at present. These views present a quiet revolution that has taken place as we entered the new millennium. These views present the picture of access of the poor to the goods and services marketed by multinational corporations (MNCs). Scholars like C. K. Prahalad, Stuart Hart, and Allen Hammond argued that this phenomenon of marketing of goods and services to a substantial number of the poor population who are (to use their words) at the 'bottom of the pyramid' or at the 'base of the pyramid' (the so-called BOP) results in alleviation of poverty, on the one hand, and, at the same time, generates profit for the business. In other words, it has been argued that a type of business involving marketing of goods and services to the poor (BOP) not only enables the business to earn a profit, the same process, they argue, also alleviates poverty. This phenomenon has been termed as "fortune at the bottom of the pyramid". In this chapter, we will examine this argument.

It may be mentioned here that in the 1990s a process of reform, involving liberalization, privatization, and globalization, has been initiated in most of the developing countries. This process of reform has taken the economies of these countries more toward a pro-capitalist economy. This process particularly gained strength with the collapse of the socialist economies of Soviet Russia and Eastern Europe. With this advancement of a capitalist ideology in the recent past, there has been a reduction in the role of government and more free play of the private sector has been witnessed in developing and developed countries of the world. Thus, in these countries, we witness some move to privatize or to promote public-private partnership that reduced the government's role in social welfare. However, the task of poverty alleviation still continued to remain a pre-rogative of the government. The main reason for this is the view point that profit maximization, the main goal of the private sector, is antitheti-cal to poverty alleviation. C.K. Prahalad observed (2007, xv) in the 'For-ward' of the book 'Business Solutions for the Global Poor':

> The idea that the private sector can contribute to the goal of pov-erty alleviation is a relatively new concept. There has long been an implicit compact between the private sector on one side and the UN, World Bank, aid agencies, national governments, and civil society on the other. They agreed, on the basis of historical evidence, that the private sector was an unlikely vehicle for dealing with poverty. The goals of profits, growth, and innovation were assumed to be contrary to the task of poverty alleviation. *The pur-pose of this book is to continue challenging this deep-seated, ideologi-cally grounded assumption.* (emphasis in the original).

Thus, the scholars propagating the "bottom of the pyramid" approach, going against conventional thinking, argued that it is possible to eradi-cate poverty through business. For instance, by selling goods and services to the "bottom of the pyramid," MNCs can earn a profit and, at the same time, poverty alleviation takes place. Alleviating poverty through a strategy of profit-earning business was a very unconventional proposition when it was suggested.

In fact, the conventional thinking of MNCs was such that they did not believe that there could be a market for their products among the poor or those who are at the bottom of the income pyramid. The typi-cal assumptions of MNCs about the BOP and the implications of such a thinking pattern, as has been articulated by Prahalad, are presented in Table 6.1.

Prahalad argued that the assumptions of MNCs about the BOP market presented in Table 6.1 are not true. We present below his major arguments in this regard briefly (Prahalad 2005, 10–16).

There is a viable market among the poor. Prahalad argued that due to inefficiencies in the market that serves the poor, people at the BOP pay

Table 6.1 The dominant logic of MNCs as it relates to BOP

Assumption	Implication
The poor are not our target customers; they cannot afford our products or services	Our cost structure is given; with our cost structure, we cannot serve the BOP market.
The poor do not have use for products sold in developed countries.	We are committed to a form over functionality. The poor might need sanitation, but cannot afford detergents in formats we offer. Therefore, there is no market in the BOP.
Only developed countries appreciate and pay for technological innovations.	The BOP does not need advanced technology solutions; they will not pay for them. Therefore, the BOP cannot be a source of innovations.
The BOP market is not critical for long-term growth and vitality of MNCs.	BOP markets are at best an attractive distraction.
Intellectual excitement is in developed markets; it is very hard to recruit managers for BOP markets.	We cannot assign our best people to work on market development in BOP markets.

Source: Prahalad, C.K. 2005. *The Fortune at the Bottom of the Pyramid*. Delhi: Pearson; p. 8.

poverty penalty for the goods and services they purchase. For instance, as Prahalad has shown that poor people living in a shanty town of Dharavi in Mumbai, India, pay as high as 5 to 25 times for goods and services, in comparison with high-income localities like Warden Road (renamed as B. Desai Road), Mumbai. Prahalad suggested that if the organized sector decides to serve this BOP market, the poor can get better-quality goods and services in much lesser a price due to skilled operation of the organized sector. Also, the organized sector will be able to make profit by serving this BOP market, which is huge. Thus, both the poor customers and the big organized sector will gain from this win-win situation.

BOP market is accessible. It has been assumed that it would be difficult for MNCs to market goods and services among the poor because of the difficulty in accessing the BOP market. But, Prahalad has pointed out that a vast majority of the poor people live in densely populated urban slums. This presents an intense distribution opportunity. The situation with the rural poor is very different in this regard. But, MNCs are engaged in experiments in finding out efficient ways of providing goods and services to the rural poor.

BOP market is brand conscious. The conventional belief is that poor people are not band conscious. On the contrary, poor people are brand and value conscious by necessity. Thus, it is a challenge for the MNCs to provide standard quality of goods and services to the poor at a lower price.

BOP market is connected. Contrary to the widespread belief, the BOP market is well connected. The penetration of cell phones among the poor households is a good example of the same. Through cell phone and TV, poor people possess shared information about goods and services with the larger community.

BOP Consumers Accept Advanced Technology Readily. There are many examples that have highlighted that poor people are using advanced technology to make informed decisions regarding economic transactions and are benefiting from the same.

Against this backdrop, there is this school of thought, which argues that the need of the hour is to promote a prominent role of the private sector in poverty alleviation. The business model suggested by this school can be called as *"Bottom of the Pyramid (BOP)" business model or BOP model.* In the section that follows we discuss this model.

It has been argued that with the opening of the closed markets in many counties due to liberalization that "The real source of market promise is not the wealthy few in the developing world, or even the emerging middle-income consumers: It is the billions of *aspiring poor* who are joining the market for the first time" (Prahalad and Hart 2002). They are at "the bottom of the pyramid (BOP)." Prahalad (2005) explains, "The distribution of wealth and the capacity to generate incomes in the world can be captured in the form of an economic pyramid. At the top of the pyramid are the wealthy, with numerous opportunities for generating high levels of income. More than 4 billion people live at the BOP on less than $2 per day." It is this BOP population whose poverty can be eradicated *profitably*, according to Prahalad.

Prahalad and Hammond (2002) made two assumptions: First, prosperity to the poor regions can come only through the direct and sustained involvement of multinational companies; and second, multinational companies can enhance their own prosperity in the process.

Prahalad and Hammond (2002) pointed out that it is not true as commonly assumed that the poor only spend on basic needs. They also spend on "luxury" items and they often pay much higher prices for most things than middle-class consumers. Thus, big corporations can have a huge market among the BOP population by offering higher quality goods at lower prices, while maintaining attractive margins. Secondly, the various perceived barriers of doing business among the poor in the developing countries are also not real. Political reform, growing openness to investment, new information technology, and communication infrastructure – especially wireless – etc. are reducing the barriers and providing access to even the poorest of city slums and rural areas.

Prahalad and Hart (2002, 6–11) elaborated on how to create a commercial infrastructure for the bottom of the pyramid market, which will result in alleviating poverty. They have mentioned the following four elements:

1. *Creating Buying Power* by providing access to credit, and increasing the earning capacity of the poor.
2. *Shaping Aspirations* through sustainable product innovations initiated in BOP population and promoted through consumer education.
3. *Improving Access* through better distribution systems and communication links for development of the BOP.
4. *Tailoring Local Solutions* to nurture local market and cultures, leverage local solutions, and generate wealth at the BOP.

It is important to note that the above-mentioned four elements of the commercial infrastructure for the bottom of the pyramid are *intertwined*.

Prahalad and Hart (2002) observed that no firm can seek their fortunes and bring prosperity to the aspiring poor alone. "Multiple players must be involved, including local governmental authorities, nongovernmental organizations (NGOs), communities, financial institutions, and other companies." However, they argue that MNCs are more favorably placed to take the lead in alleviating poverty through profit.

How poverty alleviation through profit happens? Prahalad and Hammond (2002) explained, "When MNCs provide basic goods and services that reduce cost to the poor and help improve their standard of living – while generating an acceptable return on investment – the results benefit everyone."

Poverty is multidimensional in nature. Many actors – like multinational and local businesses, entrepreneurs, civil society organizations, and governments – contribute toward business methods to work in alleviating poverty. Here, we will briefly cite some examples of cases that contributed in alleviating poverty.

The Narayana Hrudayalaya Heart Hospital in Bangalore, India presents an example of a private sector hospital making profit, while, at the same time, enables the poor to get treatment. To provide health care to the poor, this hospital attracts patients who pay the full price treatment and uses some of the profits from these services to offer at-cost or below-cost care to those who cannot afford the full fee (Rangan et al. 2007, 66–67).

Hindustan Liver Limited (HLL), a subsidiary of the big global food company, Unilever, identified rural India as a key source of growth. Project Shakti was conceptualized with that goal. Main components of Project Shakti were (a) The Shakti Entrepreneur, (b) The Shakti Vani, and (c) iShakti.

The HLL recruited underprivileged rural women as Shakti entrepreneurs and set up a team of rural sales personnel to visit, select, engage, motivate, and train them in managing business and door-to-door retailing. The HLL partnered with rural self-help groups of rural India undertaking this activity. The main thrust of this project was to enable Shakti entrepreneurs to earn an income to make it attractive to them.

Under Shakti Vani initiative, a local woman was recruited and trained as an expert in matters relating to personal and community health and hygiene. This was a communication initiative targeted at rural communities.

Under iShakti initiative, Shakti entrepreneurs were provided with a computer to create a community portal for providing information and education.

Analyzing the Shakti case, Rangan et al. (2007, 144–154) concluded that Shakti project has contributed around 10 percent of HLL's net income. On the contrary, HLL worked with women from families living below the poverty line, and for these families, Shakti improved household income from 50 to 100 percent.

The ITC Group is a large Indian private sector company. The International Business Division of ITC started exporting agricultural items like soybean meal, wheat and wheat products, lentils, shrimp, fruit pulp, and coffee. While procuring these items, ITC faced the consequences of the inefficiency of the farm-to-market supply chain. To overcome this, ITC made an innovation which is known as *e-Choupal.*

At the village level, ITC provided some selected farmers with computer and internet connectivity kiosks to provide information to farmers in the neighborhood regarding the prevailing prices of agricultural products at the markets located in the nearby town. This was to help the farmers decide when to take their produce to the nearby market for selling in order to get a better price. It also enables farmers to get a better yield by providing information about better agricultural practices. The ITC also located procurement hubs adjacent to those markets. Knowledge and information provided by the *eChoupal* are free. The farmers also are free to sell their produce to any of the various channels including the one of ITC. While this is a liberating experience for the farmer, this also pose challenges to ITC to provide a better value proposition to attract the farmers to sell their produce to ITC. It has been shown by Anupadi and Sivakumar (2007, 172–182) that this resulted in win–win situation. Overcoming various inefficiencies of the traditional system of selling produced by the farmers, *eChoupal* platform enabled the farmers to get better prices for their produce under an efficiently managed procurement system by ITC; it also enabled the ITC to procure from the farmers in a more profitable price than under the traditional system of procurement.

When a product is sold to a customer, the party selling the product makes a profit. The profit comes from the customer. In this transaction, it is the person selling the product gains. The person purchasing the product gets the utility of the product becoming poorer by the price paid for the product. Against this backdrop, C. K. Prahalad argued that when the product is made affordable to the poor and sold to them, it is not only the MNC or some other agency selling the product gains, but the poor to whom the product has been sold also gains. Prahlad has given various arguments to show how and why the purchaser of the product gains. However, some conditions should be fulfilled for the poor also to be benefitted out of this transaction. We present below this checklist

Checklist for Prospective BOP Projects

- *Consumption benefits.* Does the product provide substantial net benefits to the direct consumers?
- *Expansion of business opportunities.* Does the product create opportunities for building entrepreneurial activities, or expand opportunities to develop, create, or market locally produced goods and services?
- *Local income production in manufacturing process.* Is the product, or any component of it, locally manufactured, or produced by members of the low-income community?
- *Wage impact.* Does the local manufacture of the product generate higher wages than what prevailed in the community before?
- *Expansion of formal labor market opportunities.* Does the local manufacture of the product enhance opportunities for additional wage-earning activity that was previously unavailable?
- *Expansion of desirable wage-earning opportunities.* Does the local manufacture of the product foster opportunities for additional wage-earning activity that members of the low-income community find desirable?
- *Encouraging savings.* Does the product encourage or create opportunities to enhance saving by the consumer or others in the community?
- *Encouragement of formal banking, credit, and other business-related opportunities.* Does the product create opportunities for development of lower-cost and more comprehensive banking or other financial arrangements for consumers or other people in the low-income community?

Source: Leonard, H.B. 2007. "When Is Doing Business with the Poor Good – for the Poor: A Household and National Income Accounting Approach", in Kasturi Rangan, V., Quelch, J.A., Herrero, G. and Barton, B. (eds.) *Business Solutions for the Global Poor: Creating Social and Economic Value.* San Francisco: John Wiley & Sons; p. 370.

Leonard (2007, 372) has pointed out that "Doing Business with the Poor" need not mean only selling to the poor. It may also involve *buying from the low-income community*. Leonard (2007, 372–3) has cited the following three examples: (1) Shri Mahila Griha Udyog Lijjat Papad (SMGULP), an association of more than 40,000 members in 13 States in India comprises women from low-income communities earning by exporting *Papad* made by them to many countries. (2) Cooperative Milk Marketing Federation (CMMF), India's largest marketing organization for food products, enabled low-income communities to enhance their income by deliberately sourcing products from them. (3) SEWA Trade Facilitation Centre (STFC) enabled artisans from low-income communities to export their products by extending support, product design, and marketing assistance and thus, enhancing their income.

Leonard (2007, 370–2) also cited following two examples of applying the framework suggested by him for examining whether the BOP project can provide income to the poor: (1) Monsanto and Small Farmers in Mexico: For selling their products to small farmers in Latin America, Monsanto lacked the expertise. Hence, by partnering with Mexico Foundation for Rural Development, it could sell its products to small farmers. This intervention by farmers displaced locally produced commodities in the short run, but, in the long run, small farmers gained through increased productivity. (2) Hindusthan Lever Limited's Project Shakti (mentioned earlier): HLL was not able to sell its products to rural poor. Project Sakti involved developing local entrepreneurs as HLL agents to sell its products directly in the villages. As this reduced the distribution cost, the community benefitted from the consumption value. However, this also involved substitution of local product by imported products. However, the community benefitted from the involvement of local distributors, who could get income from this process.

It may be noted that selling to the poor by itself is not good for the poor. The important question is "under what circumstances are sales to the BOP is good *for the poor*" and what circumstances are more conducive for that. The following observation of Leonard (2007, 366) provides answer to these questions:

"Doing business with poor" is generally understood to begin with a sale of a product to a number of a low-income community, thus referencing in the first instance the *consumption* side of the transaction. But for every sale, there is both a consumption and an *income* side of transaction. Income from the sale is necessarily generated *somewhere,* and thus a key question from the perspective of the low-income community is, *Where?* Is the income side of the transaction also within the community – is the product, or some part of it, produced in the community? Or is it an import? A consumer product represents and produces value in consumption, but to the extent to which the value embodied in the product was added to the product locally, the community is better off by virtue of value on both sides of the transaction. (emphasis in the original).

The above observation by Leonard provides a good guideline to resolve when selling goods and services to the "Bottom of the Pyramid" or the poor take the shape of poverty alleviation with profits and business qualifies as benevolent business to promote social development.

CHAPTER 7

Social Welfare Business

Home-Based Care Service
for the Aged[*]

Business earns a profit while providing goods and services for the members of the society. It contributes to the growth of economy and provides employment and earning to the members of the society. However, profit maximization being the primary goal, business is not normally expected to focus on "social welfare." Of course, this does not mean that business is completely devoid of playing any welfare role. As mentioned earlier, there are claims of welfare role of business from the capitalist school (Smith 1937, 508; org.1776). On the other end, there exists the school professing Corporate Social Responsibility – that businesses "should" contribute to the society. And in-between, there is a school of "eradicating poverty through profits" by serving "the Bottom of the Pyramid" (Prahalad 2005), as discussed earlier. We have also discussed the concept of "social business," articulated by Yunus (2008), which unlike a profit-maximizing business, primarily aims at serving a social cause in a self-sustaining manner through business operations on a cost recovery basis or more.

Social welfare, on the contrary, is considered as the primary responsibility of the state. However, the extent and the nature of the welfare service to be provided by the state vary depending on the political ideology

[*]Adopted from: Mandal, K.S. 2013. "Home Based Care Service for the Aged: A Business Model of Social Welfare, Profit and Poverty Alleviation." *Indian Journal of Gerontology* 27(3):621–636.

subscribed by a particular state. For instance, a socialist state is supposed to meet all the needs, inclusive of welfare needs, of its citizens. A capitalist state is expected to provide welfare services to the most vulnerable section of the society, who fail to take the opportunities provided by the market. In a welfare state, the state takes the main responsibility of meeting the welfare needs of its citizens (Williams 1989). Nongovernmental organizations also play a role in providing social welfare services. However, they operate on a limited scale and their role is secondary to the state's role. It is under such a backdrop, that the present chapter documents an example of a business which, in the process of earning profit serves a highly needed social welfare service and, in the process, alleviates poverty of a vulnerable section of the society.

Among the various functions performed by the family, taking care of the aged is an important one. With the progress of industrialization and urbanization, many functions traditionally performed by the family are moving away from the family to other agencies. Providing care services to the aged is one such function, which is in the process of moving away from the family to an outside agency even in a nonwestern society like India. Breaking away of the Indian joint family system has added to this process. Because of the emergence of the nuclear family and small family norm, often, aged persons are in a situation to live on their own, away from their children or other younger family members – devoid of the presence of someone in the family to look after them. Secondly, as per the global trend, life expectancy is increasing in India, particularly among the upward mobile middle class and upper classes due to availability of improved medical treatments and higher standards of living. However, as people are surviving longer, the quality-of-life particularly at the advanced stage of ageing, calls for greater demand of a caregiver's service. Even when they live with their children, son, daughter-in-law, or daughter, son-in-law, or other younger members of the family, often being preoccupied with the demand of their job, they may not be available to provide the type of care service needed particularly for those who are very adversely affected by the aging process. Thus, urban nuclear families are finding it difficult to provide such engaged care services to the aged by the very members of the family. To tackle this problem, keeping the aged away from the family in an old age home is not considered as a socially desirable option by the children as well as the aged parents in Indian society. Thus, there emerged a gap in fulfilling the care needs of the aged. To meet this need, hiring fulltime home-based service of care givers for the aged caught up as a flourishing small-scale business opportunity in urban India. This service enabled the families in urban India to fulfill the care giving need of the aged at home. These service givers are women, known as ayahs (who mainly take care of the old people). Their service is less expensive than hiring a professional nurse. Demand for such services is increasing among middle-class and upper middle-class families in urban India. Agencies supplying manpower for baby seating, cooks, drivers, security personnel etc. were in existence for some time. Of late, agencies specifically supplying (wo) manpower for providing home-based care service for the aged have become an important addition in urban India. In the city of Kolkata, these centers are popularly known as ayah centers. Typically, one can hire ayahs from such centers for looking after old people at their residence, on a daily wage rate; the payment to be made at the interval of a week or ten days. Service of the ayahs can be hired for 12-hourly shifts; the day sift or night shift or for both day and night shifts as per the need. The ayah centers ensure regular supply of reliable (particularly in terms of security) (wo)manpower for this service. Regular and reliable services are very essential as the old people need this service on a regular basis. Ayah centers collect a commission from the wage paid for this service. Those willing to provide this service enroll their name with an ayah center. Often, ayah centers charge a fee for this enrolment. They are invariably women and usually without any formal training in taking care of the aged, but may acquire some on-the-job skills in looking after the aged. Ayah centers advertise their services and on receiving a call for providing such a service, supply ayahs to the families in the need of such services.

Under this arrangement, the aged member remains in the family and can receive dedicated service of a care giver – a far more favorable arrangement both for the aged person and family members, in comparison with the isolation from the family in old age homes. This arrangement of taking care of the aged at home is a socially enabling arrangement for the urban middle-class and upper middle-class families. Apart from fulfilling a felt need of urban social life, of providing care to the aged at home, this business also performs a function of poverty alleviation while earning a profit, as they create employment opportunity for marginalized women, the ayahs. Thus, it is argued that the ayah center business, providing home-based care service to the aged, is an example of a business that provides a social welfare service, does poverty alleviation by providing employment to marginalized women, and, at the same time, provides an earning to a group of entrepreneurs in the form of profit. These three functions of social welfare, poverty alleviation, and profit-making are being performed simultaneously, not so much as a part of conscious planning, but are happening in the process of addressing a business opportunity by a group of entrepreneurs.

The present study was undertaken in the context of these ayah service centers. The study specifically probed into: 1) nature of social welfare function performed by the ayah centers; 2) poverty-alleviating role of the ayah centers; and 3) nature of profit made by the ayah centers.

Data for this study were collected from the city of Kolkata, in West Bengal, India.

7.1   Method

The study was based on survey research and data were collected from greater Kolkata by interviewing ayahs (N = 300), ayah center owners (N = 60), and a knowledgeable member of the households using ayah service and/or the aged person (N = 115), with the help of interview schedules. A method was followed for selecting a representative sample of ayah centers of the city.

7.2   Findings and Discussion

Welfare Service

In this section, we discuss who hires ayahs for taking care of the aged, why they use ayah services, and how useful is this service to them?

As expected, it was found that it is mainly the small-sized nuclear families that use the ayah services for looking after the aged. The findings of this study show that family members of beneficiary families (N = 115) were not equally distributed. About 44% (N = 51) of the families had only two members, 51% (N = 58) families had 3 to 5 members, and only

5% (N = 6) families had six members. The obvious reason for opting for ayah services is the lack of manpower in the family to undertake the task of providing care to the aged. Being a nuclear family of smaller size has increased the dependence of the family on outside agencies for various functions traditionally performed by the family; the emerging trend in urban India of hiring a care giver's service for looking after the aged at home is an important component of that.

The aged persons or their household members were enquired about the reasons for availing ayah services. The earnest need of hiring an ayah for looking after the aged is obvious from the answers given by them: a) Do not have anyone to look after me (54%), b) As my children reside in their place of work somewhere else, there is no one to look after me (13%), c) My health condition requires continuous monitoring and family members lack time and capability for that (13%), d) My wife is too old and physically not capable to look after me (5%) and, and e) other reasons (15%). A somewhat tragic reality of urbanization is revealed in these responses. The main reason is that no one in the family is available to look after the aged.

Another related question asked was: what were the reasons for hiring an ayah from the ayah center and for not opting for some other arrangements? It was reported (see Table 7.1) that an important value addition that ayah centers brought in providing care to the aged is that it is of a safe

Table 7.1 Reasons for hiring ayah from ayah center

Reasons	%
	(N = 115)
Ayahs from ayah center are safe and secure	25
Ayahs know their job well	5
Ayahs from ayah center are safe and secure and they know their job well	64
Ayahs from the ayah center are safe and secure and regular as replacement is provided	3
Ayahs from ayah center are trustworthy and other reasons	3
Total	100

and secure care services nature. Safe in the sense that ayah centers are supposed to be checking the background information of the ayahs in terms of their place of residence (by checking their voter identification card or other residential address proof) and other credentials and also are supposed to take some responsibility in terms of safety (theft etc.). Another important point that was mentioned by some beneficiary households is that the ayah centers are capable of providing undisrupted care services for the aged. In case of absence of a particular ayah or discontinuation of any particular ayah, ayah centers provide immediate replacements, which is very essential for the aged, who requires continuous care services. Where 24 hours care and monitoring of the aged is needed, the ayahs are hired for day and night shifts and an ayah is supposed to leave the place of work only after handing over the charge of the aged to another ayah. Additionally, some felt that the ayahs from ayah centers are more efficient in providing care to the aged, as they gain experience from taking care of the aged in the job.

Finally, to a question "Are they satisfied with the ayah service?", about 99 percent of the beneficiary households reported that they are satisfied with the services provided by the ayah.

In summing up the findings presented in this section, it may be said that in the small nuclear families of urban India, often besides old persons, other adult family members are away in their place of work during the day or other members reside somewhere else. Thus, those families are not in a position to attend to the aged member of the family, who requires constant care and supervision. The ayah centers have emerged as a boon under such situations providing reliable services to the lonely, old members of such families. Thus, ayah centers are performing a very valuable social welfare function in our society, enabling the old to remain in the family and saving them from the isolation of being in old age homes. This is a valuable reprieve for the families availing the service of ayah centers.

This section depicted the loneliness of the life of the aged in small urban nuclear families. It may be pointed out here that the ayah service primarily takes care of meeting the physical dependency need of the aged – which in itself is a remarkable thing. But, the mental state of the lonely living of the aged needs to be addressed, which cannot be fulfilled by just providing home-based care giver services by the ayahs. Secondly, there is an important issue of affordability to arrange for home-based care services for the aged, which also needs to be addressed.

Profit

This section describes the ayah center business focusing on the socio-economic background of the ayah center owners and the type of profit they make from this business.

It is heartening to note that, in the background of male domination in most businesses, 63% of the ayah center owners were females and only 37% were males. This is due to several reasons. As this business involves dealing with ayahs who are females, running the business by a female person is convenient. Besides, this business primarily being a home-based business, women find it a convenient business to get into. Thus, ayah centers present an independent earning opportunity for those women.

Marital status of the ayah center owners (Table 7.2) shows that this business not only provides an employment opportunity to the women who are single, separated, dissertated or a widow, but it also plays a rehabilitative role for them. Such women together constitute one-third of the ayah center owners for whom this business also operates as a source of social security. Chi-squared test shows that the observed frequencies are statistically significant.

The information was collected regarding their occupation (ayah center owners) before starting an ayah center. The findings are presented in Table 7.3. Earlier, we have seen that 63% of the ayah center owners are women.

Table 7.2 Marital status of the ayah center owners

Marital status	%
	(N = 60)
Married	68
Single	22
Separated/Deserted/Widow	10
Total	100

x^2: 34.300, *df*: 2, *p*: 0.001

Table 7.3 What they did before?

What did before?	%
	(N = 60)
I was a housewife	32
I was working in public/private sector	32
I was working in a hospital/as nursing staff	13
Others	23
Total	100

x^2: 5.467, *df*: 3, *p*: 0.147

Thus, in Table 7.3 we find that half of the women owners of the ayah centers stated that they were not engaged in any paid employment and were housewives before starting the ayah center. This group of women constitutes around one-third of the ayah center owners. Another one-third of the ayah center owners said that they had been working in public or private sector jobs. Often, nursing staff of hospitals or nursing homes quit their job and became a small-time entrepreneur by starting an ayah center. Being associated with nursing homes and having a familiarity with ayahs working at nursing homes and observing the demand for ayahs for the aged patients prompted them to start an ayah center for providing ayah services for the aged. This is a common way to become an entrepreneur, which is called "industry way to entrepreneurship." However, this group of entrepreneurs constitute only a 13% of the ayah center owners.

Sizewise (number of ayahs registered for employment), ayah centers were of small-scale operations (up to 30, 37%; 31–60, 35%, and above 60, 28%). Thus, ayah centers provide a modest income. Monthly income of ayah centers is presented in Table 7.4. Around 72% of the ayah centers have reported a monthly income up to Rs 11,000. Like most income data, these data on income should be taken with due consideration, as this was self-reported and could not be verified by any other data source. However, incomes from the ayah center are not the only source of income for those families. As 63% of the ayah center owners are females, often they are not the only bread earners of their families. Income from the ayah center may be considered as only one source, often a subsidiary source of income for those families.

Table 7.4 *Monthly income from the ayah center*

Monthly income in Rs	%
	(N = 60)
Up to 6,000	37
6,001–11,000	35
11,001–2,1000	18
Above 21,000	10
Total	100

x^2:12.133, *df*: 3, *p*: 0.007

To sum it up, the interesting point is that the ayah center business is run predominantly by women; one-third of whom are either single or divorced. Thus, this business provides some sort of support to these women. This business needs little capital; hence, many housewives run this business to provide an additional source of income to their families. This business is suitable for women as this business employs women and being a home-based business, women members find it easy to run. This women friendliness of the ayah center business is a unique feature. Though in terms of earnings, this is not a very lucrative business, in terms of investment and the effort involved and the women friendliness, this can be considered an excellent type of business particularly for housewives or unmarried women. However, as this business serves an important social welfare function, there is an urgent need to bring this business under proper regulations and professionalism.

Poverty Alleviation

We have seen earlier that ayah centers provide an important social welfare service. Along with playing this welfare role, ayah centers also indirectly play a poverty-eradicating role by providing employment opportunity as ayahs to women who generally come from marginalized socio-economic backgrounds. In this section, for an understanding of this poverty-alleviating role of the ayah centers, we will take a look at a) the socio-economic background of the ayahs and b) their earning as ayahs and its impact on their families.

The ayahs (N = 300) hail from much marginalized sections of our society. Though the ayahs of our sample provide their service to the city dwellers, they often reside in the hinterland of the city and commute a long distance for work. Thus, though the ayahs of our sample provide services in the urban area, to a question as to "where they reside at present," a 27% said they resided in rural areas.

The majority of the women work as an ayah during their 30s and 40s (44%). About 18% ayahs were in their 20s, and 30% of the ayahs were in the age group of 41 years to 50 years. Only 8 per cent of the ayahs were in the 50s. Ayahs work on a 12-hour shift; therefore, older women do not find ayah job as physically suitable. Majority of ayahs had education up to secondary level.

Table 7.5 shows that though a majority of the ayahs are married, a substantial percentage of them are single, divorced, or deserted by their husband or they are a widow. The table indicates that the employment opportunity through the ayah centers helps by supporting these women in two ways. To the women who are married, ayah centers provide an additional source of income to support their needy families. For those women who do not have anyone to support, employment opportunity at the ayah center enables them to survive with their own incomes. This brings out the rehabilitative role ayah centers paly for the women in need. Chi-squared test of goodness-of-fit found the observed frequencies are statistically significant.

Table 7.5 Marital status of ayahs

Marital status	%
	(N = 300)
Married	62
Single	14
Divorced/Disserted/Widow	24
Total	100

x^2: 12.020, *df*: 2, *p*: 0.001

The author probed into the occupation of the ayahs before taking up the ayah job. Table 7.6 shows that only around one-fifth of them were employed before getting employment as ayah. Hence, for the most of them (78%), employment as ayah has provided a source of earning as they were unemployed before getting the ayah job. Thus, ayah centers provide employment opportunities to marginalized women with little education (mostly up to class X). Chi-squared test of goodness-of-fit found the observed frequencies are statistically significant.

Disadvantaged economic conditions of the ayahs are very clear also from their husband's occupational status presented in Table 7.7. A 44% of

Table 7.6 Occupation before taking up ayah job

Occupation	%
	N = 300
Unemployed	78
Cook	7
Maid servant	5
Private tuition	2
Labor	2
Sewing	3
Others	3
Total	100

x^2: 1009.560, *df*: 6, *p*: 0.001

Table 7.7 Husband's occupation

Occupation	%
	N = 300
Not applicable	44
Van rickshaw driver	11
Petty trader	16
Labor	9
Car driver	5
Salesman	2
Others	13
Total	100

x^2: 1009.560, *df*: 6, *p*: 0.001

the ayahs were deprived of a support in the form of husband's earnings – either they were deserted by their husband or their husband was unemployed or no more. Those who are fortunate to have the support of their husband's income, the husbands earned only a modest income by being employed as van rickshaw driver, petty trader, laborer, car driver, salesman etc. Chi-squared test of goodness-of-fit found the observed frequencies are statistically significant.

In response to a question about the reasons for taking up ayah job, the answers given by them have been presented in Table 7.8. This table shows that around two-fifth of the ayahs work to supplement their husband's income and the remaining three-fifth are the main bread earners of their families. It is interesting to note that in our patriarchal society, for around 60% of the women in families who work as ayahs, their income is the main source of income to support their families. Studies have also shown that among the poor, it is the income of the women of the poor households, which is spent more productively for meeting the basic needs of those families in the form of food, clothing, shelter, medical expenses, education etc. (UNICEF 1992). This brings out the significant role that this employment opportunity as ayah plays for those families. Chi-squared test of goodness-of-fit found the observed frequencies are statistically significant.

To the question on whose income supported the families of respondents (ayahs) before and after they had obtained the employment as

Table 7.8 Reasons for taking up ayah job

Reasons	%
	N = 300
To supplement husband's income	41
Husband's death/absence	20
No other earning member in the family	14
Husband income is unstable	12
Husband is unemployed	4
Others	9
Total	100

x^2:156.400, df: 5, p: 0.001

an ayah, relevant data are presented in Table 7.9. One striking change we find in this table is that there is an absolute decline in the sole role played by the husband's income in meeting household expenses after our respondents had got an employment as an ayah. After her employment as ayah, household expenditures were increasingly met either primarily from her income or both from hers and her husband's incomes. Dependence on parent's income or other sources also declined. All these are a clear sign of her economic empowerment in controlling household expenditure. Does this also enhance the social status of the ayahs in their households? Because of the complex nature of this question, we did not specifically probe this question in our study. But, some other studies are skeptical on the role of economic empowerment of poor women influencing their social status. Nevertheless, the economic empowerment of these marginalized women due to acquiring an ayah job is a thing to be appreciated.

To sum up the findings of this section, it has been shown that ayahs hail from marginalized backgrounds.[1] There is a dire need of a source of income in those families and often the ayahs were the sole bread earners in those families. Often, they did not have any alternative source of earning before they had got an ayah job. Their earning as an ayah played a vital role in running their families. Thus, we conclude that employment as an ayah indeed plays a great poverty-alleviating role.

Table 7.9 From whose income household expenditures were met before and after employment as ayah

Source of household expenditures	Before	After
	%	%
	N = 300	N = 300
Primarily my husband's income	67	1
Primarily my income	10	39
Income of both of us	13	52
Primarily parent's income	8	3
Others	2	5
Total	100	100

In this chapter, we tried to capture the picture of an emerging trend in taking care of the aged in urban India. It was found that as a part of industrialization and urbanization, changes have taken place in the social life, which has made the small nuclear families and double-earner families ill-equipped to take care of the aged parents, particularly, when fulltime care service is required by the aged. This has created a business opportunity for providing care giving services for the aged in their very homes, a much desirable option than choosing an old age home, particularly, in the context of Indian cultural norms. The study revealed that mainly small-time entrepreneurs have availed of this business opportunity. This has emerged outside of any government initiative. It was also found that this business being women-friendly, often enabled housewives or unmarried women to became a small-time entrepreneur. More importantly, ayah centers provided employment opportunity to women belonging to marginalized sections of the society and enabled their families to survive. Thus, social welfare, profit-making, and poverty alleviation are taking place through this business of ayah centers, making it a unique example of a beneficial business model.

7.3   Conclusion

To conclude, the findings of this study show that there are models of business, which serve a social cause and such business models should be promoted. However, this by no means, implicates that the state will have a reduced role in providing social welfare. Particularly, the state should play an enabling role for business models serving a social cause. For instance, in the context of ayah center business, there is an urgent need for the state to regulate the operation of the ayah centers in terms of wages paid to the ayahs, commission charged by the ayah centers, and regulating other service conditions of the ayahs. The state should ensure that ayah centers provide reliable and quality services to the aged. Most importantly, arrangements should be made to enable ayah centers provide professional services through the appropriate training of the ayah center owners and the ayahs.

Notes

1. We had a question on caste and religion of the ayahs in our question-naire. We found that ayahs were reluctant in answering that question. Hence, we decided to drop that question. However, from their surnames, we could get some idea about their caste background and found that most of the ayahs belong to the so-called lower castes and classes (scheduled castes, scheduled tribes, and other backward classes).

   Interestingly, we found that all ayahs in our sample had Hindu names. On further enquiry, we were told that a small number of ayahs belong to Muslim community, but they use a Hindu name while registering at ayah centers for better employability, particularly, in localities where the majority of the clients are Hindus.

CHAPTER 8

Benevolent Business

Poverty is too complex to be answered with one-size-fits-all approach.
                                                        —**Novogratz** *The Blue Sweater*

The government is expected to meet the social developmental needs of the people, particularly of the poor. However, often the government fails to meet the social developmental needs of the people, more so in the developing countries, due to resource limitation, maladministration and powerlessness of the poor. Nongovernmental organizations or NGOs also play a role in meeting the social developmental needs of the people. The NGOs depend on donations for funding their activities. This donation dependency often becomes a source of limitation in meeting social developmental needs of the people by the NGOs. In this background, this book suggests that along with government and the NGOs, a category of business called as benevolent business should be promoted to meet the social developmental needs in a self-sustaining manner.

As the goal of business is profit maximization, social development was not thought of to be in the agenda of business. In the previous chapters, we have discussed examples of providing social development through models of business, some being different from the usual profit maximization business or commercial business. These examples illustrate how it is possible to meet social developmental needs in a self-sustaining manner by overcoming the problem of funding social development, which is a major constraint in providing social development, particularly in the developing countries. We have also argued that by adopting the business method, it would be possible to bring efficiency in providing social development, in comparison with the social development provided by the government or NGO sector. One crucial point to be noted in the examples of the businesses we have discussed in earlier chapters is that significant innovations have been made by these business models in the conduct of business. This has been possible at times by altering some of the assumptions on which business operates in a capitalist economy. Some of these business models highlighted the altruistic aspect of human nature and serve social cause in self-sustaining manner and challenged the solely egoistic perception of human beings, as assumed under capitalist philosophy. Some of the business models discussed, like the microfinance based business, the BOP business, and the social welfare business, plays a benevolent role for the society even being primarily driven by egoistic values. We have clubbed all these business models under a category of "benevolent business" because these business models, whether based on altruistic or egoistic values, promote benevolence of the society. Below, we have identified some of the important principles followed by these benevolent business models. It may be mentioned that as the principles of benevolent business have been identified from business models which differ widely and at times they differ in their basic assumptions about human nature, some of the principles may not be applicable to all business models we have discussed. But we have clubbed them together as all these principles resulted into business having beneficial impact on the society. These principles will be helpful for designing a benevolent business based on these wining principals. Thus, we discuss below these "Principals of Benevolent Business".

8.1   Principles of Benevolent Business

Benevolent Business Serves Social Cause

Goal of benevolent business is to serve a social cause and not just to earn and maximize profits. However, some models of benevolent businesses may be guided by the profit maximization goal but social cause gets served in the process. There are so many social problems in the society. Instead of depending only on the government or NGOs to solve those problems, one can think of business ideas revolving around those problems and try to solve those problems in a self-sustaining manner through business. For instance, as we have seen in the example of Nutrimix social business, the goal of that business is to mitigate the problem of child malnutrition by selling Nutrimix to the poor at a price affordable to them at the same time maintaining self-sustenance. The bottom line of this business has been that how many children have been impacted in mitigating malnutrition by this business and not how much profit this business could make. Of course, this does not mean making profit is less important, because if this business runs at a loss, it would require to be closed, defeating the very purpose of mitigating the problem of malnutrition.

The Guiding Principle of Benevolent Business is Compassion and Not Profit Maximizing

When a feeling of compassion toward the marginalized section rather than the profit motive becomes the guiding principle of business, the entire scenario of conducting business changes. This has been exemplified by the Aravind case. It is this sense of compassion that has guided Aravind to make innovations providing high-volume and best-quality treatment at reduced cost to every patient, irrespective of the paying capacity of the patients.

In fact, benevolent businesses should be based not only on a feeling of compassion; it often takes into account the faith in the goodness of human beings. That such a perception is not a utopia and has solid foundation have been proved by offering loans to the poor without collateral under microfinance. The microfinance revolution all over the world has demonstrated that by its impressive record of loan recovery, much better than the profit maximizing commercial banking system providing loan only against collateral.

Benevolent Business Does Not Pay any Dividend

It is commonly assumed that the goal of business is to earn a profit, and the profit goes to the owner of the business or the shareholders of the business. It is also assumed that the goal of business is to maximize profit for increasing the monetary gains of the owners of the business or the shareholders of the business. In the commercial businesses, profit maximization is often achieved by various methods such as by enhancing the price, by giving less for the price charged, by paying less to the workers, or by hiring less-qualified workers at a lower wage, and using inferior quality materials in producing goods for reducing costs and getting higher margins, etc. Adopting these types of practices under the urge to maximize profit is obviously not beneficial for the society.

If a business is not a dividend paying business, then the question of maximizing profit does not arise. Thus, benevolent businesses need not adopt the above-mentioned harmful practices. On the contrary, as a benevolent business is not under the urge of maximizing profits, it can offer better services at a reduced cost, benefitting the poor. For instance, when Nutrimix Social Business strived to increase its impact in mitigating malnutrition, attempts were made to spread the use of Nutrimix; the resultant increased production giving an economy of scale also helped making Nutrimix more affordable to the poor. Thus, the Nutrimix social business could cut down the price of Nutrimix. The Arvind Eye Care System adopted a policy of "give more for less," the exact opposite of a commercial business, which usually tries to "give less for more" for profit maximization.

Thus, not paying dividend facilitates a benevolent business to do more good to the society. For instance, the surplus generated by Nutrimix social business helped in financing its expansion by setting up additional units thus making greater impact in mitigating child malnutrition. Similar practice was followed by Aravind Eye Care System also, '. . . not only is the Aravind Eye Care System self-sufficient in terms of operational income and expenditure, but it also takes care of capital expenditure for all expansion and new units' (Prahalad 2005, 269). It may be mentioned that the workers and managerial staff of a benevolent business earn a salary as per the prevailing market rate and not less. Thus, if we just imagine of a world where businesses need not pay any dividend, it would be a very different world. The world would have been a much better place to live in with healthy business practices and less inequality.

The Capital for Starting a Benevolent Business Comes from Loan, Donation, Grant, or Some Other Similar Source

Business requires capital for investment. The most common way of a commercial business to raise capital is by selling shares in the market.

Shareholders invest for earning from dividends. That is the main incentive for shareholders to invest in a business. When not paying dividend is a principle of a benevolent business, this type of business would find it difficult to get initial capital to start the business. Thus, a benevolent business would need to depend on donation or loan on easy terms to be paid back after it become a viable business. Attempts are being made by some trusts and some other organizations to create a fund for benevolent businesses. Yunus Centre set up by Muhammad Yunus is actively engaged in promoting social business, a benevolent business. Some attempts are being made to facilitate benevolent businesses by making a fund available for them, like "patient capital" under the initiative of Jacqueline Novogratz (2009, 213–234). Those who donate to NGOs would be more interested in donating to a social business for a greater impact of their donations. This is because money given to charity has only one life whereas money invested in social business gets multiple life as it comes back and gets reinvested in serving the social cause. The mechanism of microcredit also enables poor people to get access to a small capital for taking up a microbusiness to resolve their poverty. Thus, some alternative mechanisms have been invented that would enable a benevolent business to obtain its capital for starting a business. However, availability of capital to start a benevolent business still remains one main hurdle in the way of spreading of benevolent business.

Making Goods and Services Affordable to the Poor Is One Important Goal of Benevolent Businesses

Making goods and services affordable to the poor serves in catering to the interests of the poor. Goods and services can be made affordable to the poor in diverse ways.

One important way is frugal entrepreneurship or innovations to make goods and services affordable to the poor and cost cutting (more on this under next sub-heading).

Another way of making goods and services affordable to the poor is by selling goods and services designed in a way, which is affordable and easily available to the poor. Selling goods in smaller quantity, packaging in sachets, at a price affordable to the poor is an example of such strategy followed by BOP model.

Through selling goods to the poor by enabling them to buy the product, at times, serves a social purpose. For instance, Hindustan Lever Limited, the largest soap producer in India, projected promoting handwashing with soap at an affordable price among the poor as a preventive behavior for diarrheal disease in India (Prahalad 2005, 207–235). One advantage of this approach is that as poor people are numerous, making goods and services affordable to them gives a huge market and provides an economy of scale that also facilitates surplus generation and viability of the business, while also serving a social cause.

Further, as some benevolent businesses do not pay any dividend and the profit is ploughed back into the business, this facilitates the process of providing better quality of goods and services at an affordable price to the poor.

Profit maximizing businesses, on the other hand, would instead of making high-quality goods affordable tend to charge higher prices with quality improvements. As opposed to the policy of profit maximizing business that strive to "give less for more," benevolent businesses follow the principle of "giving more for less." Careful studies of benevolent businesses suggest that the success of this business depends on the ability in proving high-quality goods and services at affordable prices.

Aravind converted the very process of providing high-volume services into high-quality services through appropriate innovations involving more efficient utilization of the expertise of the doctors and better utilization of nursing services at a reduced cost.

Benevolent Business Practices Cost Cutting and Frugal Entrepreneurship

Being a pro-poor business, benevolent businesses usually cannot be an extravagant business and always attempt to cost cutting and strive to be innovative to reduce the costs of goods and services provided to its beneficiaries. The obvious reason for adopting cost cutting and frugal entrepreneurship is to make goods and services affordable, particularly, to the poor. Aravind Eye Care System is a very good example of how through various innovative practices, it could make best utilization of the expertise of doctors and nursing staff at a reduced cost and could provide better quality free treatment to the majority of its patients, but still could make a profit.

Further, for making better types of treatment affordable to the poor, Aravind endeavored into manufacturing the intraocular lens (IOL) at highly reduced prices to offer modern cataract surgery to the poor for a minimal fee or free of cost.

Nutrimix Social Business developed a protein and calorie dense supplementary food for the children which is less than one-fifth of the cost of the baby food marketed by multinational corporations.

Benevolent Business Tends to Be a High-volume Business

As benevolent businesses more often aim at reaching the poor who are numerous, they would usually need to be a high-volume business. Making goods and services affordable to the poor would necessitate to strive for a high-volume business, which also facilitates affordability by promoting economies of scale. For instance, with the increase in sales volume, it was possible to reduce the price of Nutrimix, which facilitated to expand its market further.

However, it should be mentioned that as benevolent businesses often may have initial capital constraints, it would start small and likely to expand gradually. Arvind started as an 11-bed hospital at a private residential home and gradually emerged as a provider of treatment to the highest number of patients at most affordable prices in the World.

Benevolent Businesses May Cross Subsidize Goods and Services to the Poor

Cross subsidy and differential pricing are important policy instruments followed by benevolent businesses for providing services to the poor. Aravind is a good example for the same. Profit maximization businesses follow the policy of providing goods and services to those who can pay. Profit maximizing business aims at those who have purchasing power. Defying those rules of profit maximization business, benevolent businesses provide goods and services to the needy, irrespective of their purchasing power through cross subsidy or differential pricing in a self-sustaining manner.

Benevolent Business Helps the Poor to Overcome Poverty

A business which may or may not aim at serving a social purpose but is owned by the poor and helps the poor to overcome poverty by generating income to them may be considered as benevolent business. The poor may undertake income generating activities through microcredit or forming a cooperative. Unlike a commercial business which aims at giving higher dividend to its owners, a cooperative business, for instance, may aim at giving maximum price to the producers by providing high quality products to the consumers by manufacturing value-added products. Thus, benefiting both the producers and the consumers. As for example, the milk cooperative Amul worked hard to provide high quality product to the customers at the same time provided maximum price of the milk to the farmers, not for maximize dividend as is done under commercial business. It achieved this by manufacturing value-added products to give higher price to the farmers. Further, benevolent business helps the poor to overcome poverty also by providing better quality product and service at a reduced price.

To sum up, a benevolent business is a business that aims at serving a social cause in a self-sustaining manner. The guiding principle of benevolent business is compassion and not profit maximization. This business may not pay any dividend. The benevolent business should be self-sustaining or more. Any profit made by this business does not go to any individual, but ploughed back into the business for serving a social cause better. Benevolent business gets its capital from donation, loan or from some other sources. It practices cost cutting and frugal entrepreneurship and strives to make goods and services affordable to the poor, including providing free service to the needy through cross subsidy. It strives to become a high volume business expanding to cover more people, particularly the poor. Benevolent business aims at alleviating poverty.

It may be mentioned that in our examples of benevolent business we have included microfinance based business, BOP business and social welfare business which are profit maximization business but serves social cause in the process of earning a profit. Thus, they are examples of benevolent business. However, being profit maximization business some of the characteristics mentioned above may be only partly applicable to those business models.

Presently it is assumed that promoting social development is primarily the responsibility of the government. Apart from the government, the NGOs also play a role, a subsidiary role than the government, in promoting social development. On the other hand, business sector which aims at earning a profit and maximizing profit is not expected to play any role in promoting social development. We have shown in our preceding discussion that apart from just profit maximizing business, there exist some different types of business models. We have discussed examples of some such business models. The business models we have discussed either specifically aim at promoting social development or in the process of earning a profit they alleviate poverty or serve social causes. These business models bring benevolence of society. Thus, we have called these business models as the models of benevolent business. We recommend that along with the government and the NGOs, the benevolent business should be promoted for the advancement of social development. By promoting social development in a self-sustaining manner, the benevolent business models will be helpful in overcoming the problem of scarcity of fund for social development. This will be particularly helpful for the developing countries which suffer from resource crunch in meeting the social developmental needs. This will also be a way out of the situation where due to the advancement of policy of liberalization government is increasingly limiting its role in social development. Finally, as unlike the government and the NGO sector, business sector is exposed to market competition, the benevolent business will be more efficient than the government and the NGO sector in promoting social development. Thus, we suggest that the government, the NGOs and the benevolent business jointly should be engaged in the promotion of social development.

References

Anupindi, R., and Sivkumar, S. 2007. "ITC's e- Choupal: A Platform Strategy for Rural Transformation", in Quelch, J., Rangan, V.K., Barton, B., Herrero, G. (eds.) *Business Solutions for the Global Poor.* John Wiley & Sons, Inc., San Francisco.

Arndt, H.W. 1983. "The Trickle-Down Myth." *Economic Development and Cultural Change* 32 (1):1–10.

Bandyopadhyay, T. 2016. *Bandhan – The Making of a Bank.* Penguin, Gurgaon.

Banerjee, A., Duflo, E., Glennester, R., and Kinnan, C. 2015. "The Miracle of Microfinance? Evidence from a Randomized Evaluation", *American Economic Journal: Applied Economics* 7(1):22–35.

Beejal, K., Vijay, M.R., Bharali, R., Karothiya, R., and Samanta, S. 2008. Business Plan for Low-cost Baby Food (Nutrimix). A project report submitted to Indian Institute of Management Calcutta and Child in Need Institute (mimio.).

Birchall, J. 2003. *Rediscovering the Cooperative Advantage: Poverty Reduction through Self-help.* International Labour Office, Geneva.

Brainard, L., and LaFleur, V. 2006. "The Private Sector in the Fight against Global Poverty", in Brainard, L. (ed.) *Transforming the Development Landscape: The Role of the Private Sector.* Brookings Institution Press, New York.

Dees, J.G. 1998. "Enterprising Nonprofits," *Harvard Business Review*, The January February 1998 issue, 55–57.

Dees, J.G. 2012. "A Tale of Two Cultures: Charity, Problem Solving, and the Future of Entrepreneurship," *Springer Science + Business Media* B.V. 2012, Published online: 17 August 2012. link.springer.com/*arti cle/10.1007%2Fs10551-012-1412-5*.

Florence, P.S. 1972. "Cooperatives" in *International Encyclopedia of Social Sciences*, Vol. 3and 4, The Macmillan Company & The Free Press, New York.

Goulet, D.1992. "Development: Creator and Destroyer of Values." *World Development* 20(3):467–475.

Grember, K. V. et al. 2017. *2017 Global Hunger Index: The inequalities of hunger*, International Food Policy Research Institute, Washington.

Hewavitharana, B. 2004. "Framework for Operationalizing the Buddhist Concept of Gross National Happiness" in Ura, K., Galay, K. (eds.) *Gross National Happiness and Development.* Proceedings of the First International Seminar on Operationalization of Gross National Happiness. The Centre for Bhutan Studies, Thimpu (mimio.).

Hunt, D. 1989. *Economic Theories of Development. An Analysis of Competing Paradigms.* Harvester Wheatsheaf, Hertfordshire.

Ingham, B. 1993. "The Meaning of Development: Interactions between 'New' and 'Old' Ideas." *World Development* 21 (11):1773–1786.

International Cooperative Alliance. 1995. "Statement on the Cooperative Identity", Report of the 31st Congress, Manchester, in Review of International Cooperation, 88.3.

Kurien, V. 2005 (as told to Gouri Salvi). *I Too Had a Dream*. Roli Books, New Delhi.

Leonard, H.B. 2007. "When Is Doing Business with the Poor is Good for the Poor: A Household and National Income Accounting Approach", in Quelch, J., Rangan, V.K., Barton, B., Herrero, G. (eds.) *Business Solutions for the Global Poor.* John Wiley & Sons, Inc., San Francisco.

Marx, K. 1977; org.1859. 'Preface.' *A Contribution to the Critique of Political Economy*. Progress Publisher, Moscow.

Mehta, P.K., and Shenoy, S. 2012. *Infinite Vision: How Aravind Became the World's Greatest Business Case for Compassion.* Collins Business, Noida.

Microcredit Summit Campaign. 2016. http://www.microcreditsummit.org/what-is-microfinance2.html.

Nandi Foundation. 2011. *HUNGaMA Fighting Hunger & Malnutrition: The HUNGaMA Survey Report – 2011.* Nandi Foundation, Hyderabad. https://www.cse.iitb.ac.in/~sohoni/TD604/HungamaBKDec11LR.pdf.

Novogratz, J. 2009. *The Blue Sweater: Bridging the Gap between Rich and Poor in an Interconnected World*. Rodale, New York.

Prahalad, C.K. 2005. *The Fortune at the Bottom of the Pyramid: Eradicating poverty through profits.* Wharton School Publishing/Pearson Education, Delhi.

Prahalad, C.K., and Hammond, A. 2002. "Serving the World's Poor Profitably", *Harvard Business Review.* September 2002, 1–16. https://hbn.org/2002/09/serving-the-worlds-poor-profitability.

Prahalad, C.K., and Hart, S.L. 2002. "The Fortune at the Bottom of the Pyramid", *Strategy + Business.* Issue 26, 1–16.

Prahalad, C.K. 2007. In the 'Forward' of the book, *Business Solutions for the Global Poor: Creating Social and Economic Value.* John Wiley and Sons, SanFrancisco.

Quelch, J., Rangan, V.K., Barton, B., Herrero, G. (eds.) 2007. *Business Solutions for the Global Poor: Creating Social and Economic Value.* John Wiley and Sons, SanFrancisco.

Sachs, J. 2012. "Introduction" in Helliwell, J., Layard, R., and Sachs, J. (eds.) *World Happiness Report.* Adopted by the UN member states at Rio+20 summit in Rio de Janeiro in June 2012. http://www.earth.columbia.edu/sitefiles/file/Sachs%20Writing/2012/World%20Happiness%20Report.pdf.

Salamon, L.M., Anheier, H.K., List, R., Toepler, S. Sokolowski, S.W., and Associates.1999. *Global Civil Society Dimensions of the Nonprofit Sector.* The Johns Hopkins Center for Civil Society Studies, Baltimore.

Sen, A. 1983. "Development: Which Way Now." *Economic Journal* 93(372): 745–762.

Sen, A. 2003. "Radical Needs and Moderate Reforms" in Dreze, J., and Sen, A. (eds.) *Indian Development: Selected Regional Perspectives.* Oxford University Press, New Delhi.

Singh, Y. 1973. *Modernization of Indian Tradition.* Thomson Press (India) Limited, New Delhi.

Smith, A. 1937; org. 1776. *An Inquiry into the Nature and Causes of the Wealth of Nations.* The Modern Library, New York.

Sriram, M.S. 2011. *Profit or Purpose: The Dilemma of Social Enterprises.* Working Paper No. 2011-08-02, August 2011, Indian Institute of Management, Ahmadabad (mimeo.).

Thinley, L.J. Y. 1999. "Values and Development: "Gross National Happiness" ", in Kinga, S. et al. (eds.) *Gross National Happiness: A set of discussion papers.* The Centre for Bhutan Studies, Thimpu (mimeo.).

UNICEF. 1992. *Support to Women's Economic Activities and Income Generation in the 1990s.* UNICEF, New York.

United Nation Development Program. 1992. *Human Development Report 1992.* Oxford University Press, New York.

Williams, F. 1989. "Perspective of Welfare: The Existing, but Inadequate Theoretical Basis of Social Policy", in *Social Policy: A Critical Introduction.* Policy Press, New York.

World Commission on Environment and Development (Brundtland Commission). 1987. *Our Common Future.* Oxford University Press, New York.

Yunus, M. 2007. *Banker to the Poor: The Story of the Grameen Bank.* Penguin, New Delhi.

Yunus, M. 2008. *Creating a World without Poverty: Social Business and the Future of Capitalism.* Subarna, Dhaka.

Yunus, M. 2010. *Building Social Business - The New Kind of Capitalism that Serves Humanity's Most Pressing Needs.* PublicAffairs, New York.

Index

www.ingramcontent.com/pod-product-compliance
Lightning Source LLC
Chambersburg PA
CBHW062042200326
41519CB00017B/5108